CROSS STITCH
Antique
Style
SAMPLERS

Jane Greenoff

David and Charles

To Bill, James and Louise
with love always

A DAVID & CHARLES BOOK
David & Charles is a subsidiary of F+W (UK) Ltd.,
an F+W Publications Inc. company

First published in the UK in 2005
Reprinted 2006 (twice)
Text and designs Copyright © Jane Greenoff 2005
Photography and layout Copyright © David & Charles 2005

Distributed in North America
by F+W Publications, Inc.
4700 East Galbraith Road
Cincinnati, OH 45236
1-800-289-0963

Jane Greenoff has asserted her right to be identified as author of this work
in accordance with the Copyright, Designs and Patents Act, 1988.

A catalogue record for this book is available from the British Library.
ISBN 0 7153 1830 6

Executive commissioning editor Cheryl Brown
Desk editor Ame Verso
Executive art editor Ali Myer
Art editor Prudence Rogers
Project editor Lin Clements
Photography Simon Whitmore, Karl Adamson and Pete Canning (antique samplers)

Printed in Singapore by KHL Printing Co Pte Ltd
for David & Charles
Brunel House   Newton Abbot   Devon

Visit our website at www.davidandcharles.co.uk

David & Charles books are available from all good bookshops; alternatively you can contact our Orderline
on (0)1626 334555 or write to us at FREEPOST EX2110, David & Charles Direct, Newton Abbot TQ12 4ZZ, UK
(no stamp required UK mainland).

The Cross Stitch Guild

The Cross Stitch Guild was formed in March 1996 and quickly became a worldwide organization with a committed and enthusiastic body of members – over 2,000 in the first six months of operation. As word spreads it is clear that many cross stitch and counted thread addicts around the world are delighted to have a Guild of their own. The CSG has received an extraordinary level of support from designers, retailers, manufacturers and stitchers. Guild members receive a full-colour bi-monthly magazine, *Stitch That with Jane Greenoff*, with cross stitch designs, counted thread patterns, new products and news and information. The CSG also supplies cross stitch kits, gold-plated needles, stitchers' gifts and Jane Greenoff's classes. There is now a comprehensive website for members and non-members, with the stitchers' market open to all:
www.thecrossstitchguild.com
For more information and a catalogue contact: CSG HQ, Yells Yard,
Cirencester Road, Fairford, Gloucestershire, GL7 4BS, UK.
Tel: from the UK 0800 328 9750; from overseas +44 1285 713799.

◄ *(Frontispiece, previous page): The picture shows two red samplers – an antique sampler by Catherine Archer and my Bristol Orphanage Sampler (see page 54). I was lucky enough to find the little sampler book, complete with the contents, stitched by a girl called Alice Flower. She had drawn each project or technique beautifully in fine ink and then worked the technique on the opposite page. The book included a small marking sampler, a baby's bonnet, a tiny nightdress and any number of patches and darns – a real treasure!*

Contents

Introduction   4

A Brief History of Samplers   6

Back to Basics   10

House Samplers   14

Alphabet Samplers   22

Map Samplers   30

Darning Samplers   38

Spot Motif Samplers   46

Red Samplers   54

Berlin Woolwork Samplers   62

Victorian Sentiments   70

Band Samplers   78

Stitch Library   88

Additional Charts   98

Finishing & Making Up   100

Caring for Antique Samplers   102

Further Reading   103

Acknowledgments   103

Suppliers   104

Index   105

Introduction

This is a book I have always wanted to write! From the beginning of my love affair with embroidery, and particularly with the counted thread variety, I have had a passion for samplers. I say passion advisedly because I have been known to have real physical pain when walking around an exhibition of antique samplers where they are either not for sale or have such high value as to be completely out of the reach of us ordinary mortals!

Since 1985 I have been collecting antique embroidery, particularly samplers, and continue to search for more of these treasures. And treasure is what they are – a child stitched one of my map samplers in 1815 – the year that Wellington won the Battle of Waterloo! I still find it difficult to imagine children as young as eight, working away at some fine embroidery for hours at a time. When you consider poor nutrition, no electricity, rough needles and complete lack of equipment it is even more incredible that these beautiful pieces of stitching were completed at all! During the 20 years I have been designing and stitching, I still love to work traditional samplers on unbleached linen, attempting to emulate the standard and excellence of school-age children.

I have used my collection of antique samplers as inspiration for this book but have not reproduced them in chart form. Instead I have designed and stitched a variety of samplers to echo the feel and atmosphere of these old embroideries, often using pastel shades to create that wonderful faded and aged appearance, although the original samplers were not stitched with pastel colours of course but have faded over the passage of time.

I hope that you enjoy stitching the samplers and the other smaller projects in this book and in the process create some beautiful heirlooms of your own.

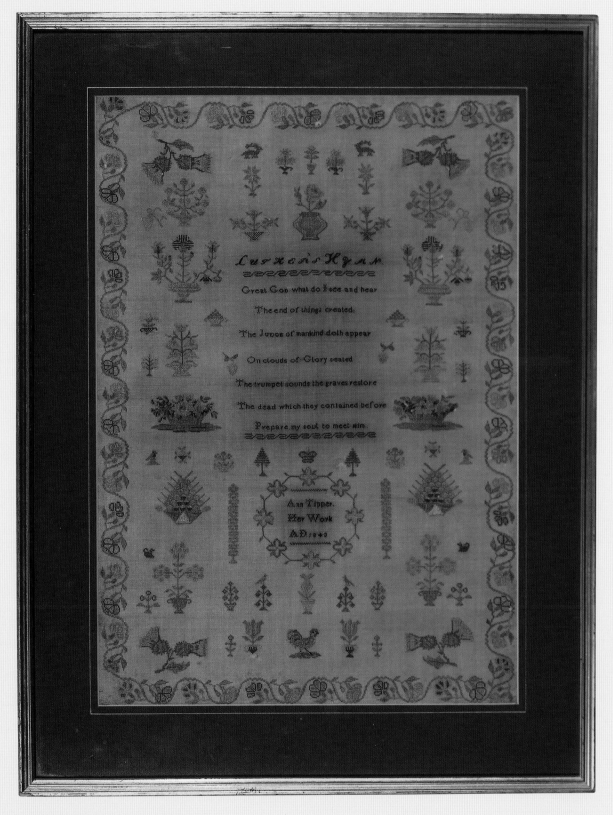

▲ *I can remember the day we bought this sampler as if it were yesterday. It was our very first antique purchase, bought for me by my husband, Bill, instead of an eternity ring! Unfortunately it had been washed and not by an expert and there are some colour runs that we could not remove. Ann Tipper worked the sampler on very fine linen and included the words for Luther's hymn. The stitches are tiny and worked very neatly indeed.*

A Brief History of Samplers

◇◇◇◇◇◇◇◇◇◇◇◇◇◇◇◇◇◇◇◇◇◇◇◇◇◇◇◇

▲ *This colourful motif paper sampler was purchased at a stitching show in London. It is very unusual to see motifs stitched on paper; these were worked in cross stitch and satin stitch in a pretty range of colours. The sampler, dated 1893, is awaiting restoration.*

The term 'sampler' comes from the Latin *exemplum*, meaning an example to be followed, a pattern or model. It is believed that although the earliest dated samplers and references to them come from the 16th century, they were stitched long before this time – simple embroideries on linen have been found in the tombs of the Pharaohs.

Some of the earliest samplers from the 16th century, typically band samplers, included a huge variety of stitches. They were made from long, thin strips of linen and were not intended to be decorative but to act as a reference to stitchers, and were kept rolled up in a drawer to be referred to as necessary. These now very valuable treasures demonstrate the skill, diligence and patience of the embroiderers and leave us in awe of their talent. We also have to remember that the fabric had to be woven and the threads dyed before the stitching began in earnest.

The first known dated English sampler was made by Jane Bostocke in 1598 to celebrate the birth of her daughter Alice Lee, and

This Mary Fowler sampler was bought from a friend, partly because Fowler was my maiden name and also because it is such an unusual and fine early example stitched in 1725. As part of its restoration it was stitched on to washed linen and then mounted on acid-free card.

This sampler by Christina Wood of Nottingham was worked on linen with a striking castle, lovely spot motifs and a strawberry border. Christina did not date her sampler but she was born in November 1816.

you can see this exquisite embroidery at the Victoria and Albert Museum in London. This work, although 16th century, is not a band sampler but more a spot motif sampler, covered with random motifs in a variety of stitches and shades, and including metal threads, pearls and beads.

Later in the 17th century the style changed to spot samplers, which included random motifs worked in coloured threads. These could be used on costumes, bed hangings or other furnishings. During this period printed pattern books became available, so samplers lost some of their use as reference works. It is probably true that this was the golden era for sampler making as the use of motifs and quality of stitching has never been bettered.

From the mid-18th century onwards, it became more common for young girls to work samplers as part of their education. Alphabet samplers, pictorial designs including houses and animals, decorative borders, poems and prayers became common and today represent the popular image of the sampler. Marking samplers included various

▲ *I often wonder who the people in this Victorian picture were. Absent But Not Forgotten was worked on stitching paper and was spotted, examined and paid for in the ten minutes that my husband was in a shop in Truro!*

alphabets in reversible stitches, crowns and coronets, which could be used to mark the household linens of the aristocracy. Some samplers contained pious verses or religious symbols and others taught geography in the form of embroidered maps, or mathematics as almanacs or multiplication tables.

During Victorian times samplers became more pictorial and metamorphosed into decorative articles to be hung on the parlour walls by proud parents, or in the case of the sampler shown above, by rather dour Victorians! These would generally be worked in cross stitch or tent stitch and

▲ *I bought this red French sampler at a Talent for Textiles sale near Bath, England. Stitched for a mother, it was worked on double canvas with the background left unstitched. This red sampler is not dated but must have been stitched after 1860 as that is when double canvas was first available.*

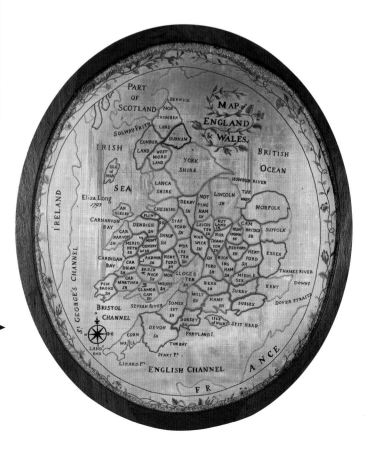

This map of England and Wales, ➤ *stitched on silk in 1793 by Eliza Long, is in urgent need of restoration. The counties are all marked and the map has the addition of a decorative compass and a lovely rosebud border.*

often included the child's name and age. With the high child mortality at the time, the death of a sibling or other family member was commonplace and so a very Victorian theme became more common, that of the mourning sampler, possibly worked in large amounts of black and occasionally including stitching done with the hair of the deceased!

Throughout the centuries the creation of samplers has given much pleasure, not only to the stitchers but to those admiring the work, and for some it becomes a totally absorbing pastime. Below is an extract from a poem written around 1865 when Berlin woolwork was at its height and yet I am sure many stitchers (and certainly their partners) would recognize the sentiment today.

Oh lord, preserve me from a wife with fancy work gone wild,

With hands that never do aught else for husband or for child.

Our clothes are rent, our bills unpaid, our house is in disorder,

All because my lady wife has taken to embroider!

(Anon.)

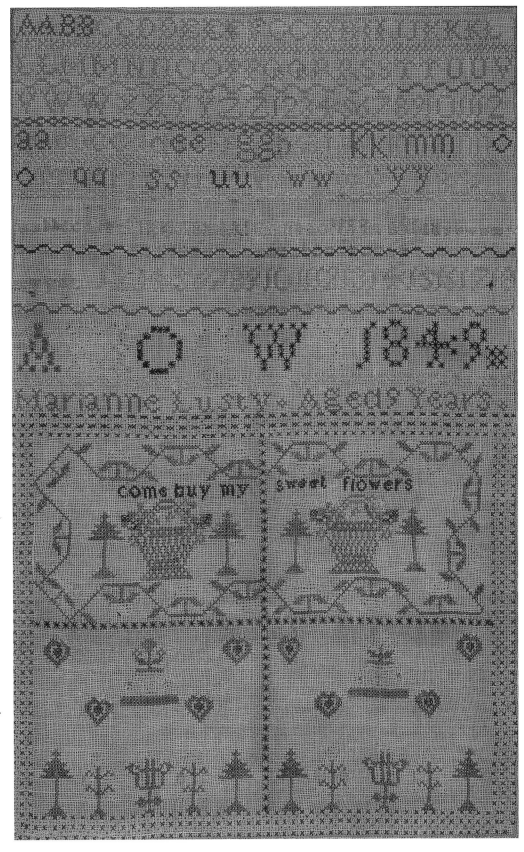

▲ *This lovely sampler was worked by Marianne Lusty in 1849. I bought it because I loved the way she had incorporated the words 'come buy my sweet flowers' in the middle of the sampler. It is worked mainly in blues and antique golds and I love it.*

Back to Basics

◇◇◇◇◇◇◇◇◇◇◇◇◇◇◇◇◇◇◇

This section describes the basic materials and equipment needed, how to use charts, prepare fabric and start stitching. It also describes the basic techniques for counted embroidery, with some useful cross stitching tips. See the Stitch Library pages 88–97 for working all other stitches.

Materials and Equipment

Fabrics

The fabrics used for counted cross stitch are woven with the same number of threads or blocks to 2.5cm (1in) in both directions. The warp and weft are woven evenly so when a stitch is formed it appears as a square or part of a square. When choosing fabrics for counted cross stitch, the thread count differentiates between the varieties available – the higher the count, the more threads or stitches to 2.5cm (1in) and the finer the fabric.

Evenweaves, including linens, are woven singly, which means single threads can be withdrawn, making them suitable for withdrawn and pulled thread work. They are made from various fibres and mixtures and in different colours, counts and bands.

Aida fabric is designed for cross stitch and is woven in blocks rather than singly. It is available in 8, 11, 14, 16, 18 and 20 blocks to 2.5cm (1in) and in many colours. Aida is now available made from linen thread.

Threads

The most commonly used thread for counted embroidery is stranded cotton (floss) but there are many other types now available. I have used stranded cotton (floss) with the addition of metallic threads for some projects.

Needles

Use blunt tapestry needles for counted cross stitch. The commonest sizes used are 24 and 26 but this depends on the project and personal preference. I always use a gold-plated needle, finding the nickel variety less satisfactory. Avoid leaving a needle in the fabric unless it is gold plated or it may cause marks.

Scissors

Use dressmaker's shears for cutting fabric and a small, sharp pair of pointed scissors for cutting embroidery threads. I keep mine on a ribbon around my neck, which means I always know where they are!

Frames and Hoops

These are not essential but if you do use one, choose one large enough to hold the complete design, to avoid marking the fabric and flattening your stitches. All the designs in this book, with the exception of the darning sampler, were stitched without a frame or hoop.

Using This Book

✔ Throughout this book, I have used Zweigart linens, which I think are the best needlework fabrics. When you are going to spend many hours working on your sampler, it is worthwhile using the best available. Linen is the most appropriate fabric for the creation of samplers, although I have indicated where you could substitute Aida fabric if preferred.

✔ I have used colour charts with symbols so you can visualize the designs more easily. You could photocopy and enlarge the charts for your own use.

✔ All the designs have been stitched in DMC stranded embroidery cotton (floss) unless stated otherwise. Anchor colour equivalents have been given where possible (in brackets).

✔ Measurements are given in metric with imperial conversions in brackets – work with one or the other.

✔ Most of the designs use just cross stitch and backstitch but the band samplers are more adventurous so refer to the Stitch Library, starting on page 88, for how to work the stitches used.

✔ Each chapter has a large sampler project, with full instructions and chart, followed by one or two smaller, quick-to-work projects that use parts of the large chart or have their own chart on pages 98–99.

Techniques

Preparing Fabric

Press the fabric before you begin stitching and trim the selvage or any rough edges. When working with linen or linen mixtures, sew a narrow hem around all raw edges to preserve them for hemstitching when the project is completed. Avoid using masking tape as the adhesive creeps and attracts grime. Work from the middle of the fabric and middle of the chart where possible to ensure your design is centred on the fabric. Find the middle of the fabric by folding it in four and pressing lightly. Work lines of tacking (basting) stitches following a fabric thread to mark the folds. When working a band sampler it is also a good idea to tack (baste) a line down each side of the outermost stitches on the first completed band, to indicate where the bands should start and stop.

Working from Charts

The designs in this book are worked from charts and are counted designs. The charts are in colour with a black or white symbol to aid colour identification and allow you to photocopy for your own use. Each square, both occupied and unoccupied, represents two threads of linen or one block of Aida unless stated otherwise. Each occupied square equals one stitch. I have avoided using fractional stitches as much as possible as traditional sampler makers did not use them.

When looking at a chart, try to plan your stitching direction. If you count across the shortest distances of empty fabric each time you will avoid counting mistakes. To prevent serious counting errors, rule a line on the chart to match the centre using a coloured pen. You can turn your work and the chart upside-down if you prefer to work towards you, but never turn halfway – your stitches will end up facing the wrong way! I make a copy of a chart so that I can lightly colour it in as I proceed, to avoid looking at the wrong section.

Calculating Design Size

Being able to calculate the eventual size of a design means that you will be able to decide how much fabric you need for a particular project or whether a design will fit a specific card aperture or picture frame.

Calculate design size as follows: count the number of stitches in each direction on the chart and then divide these numbers by the stitch count of your fabric.

> For example:
> A design on 14-count Aida of 140 stitches x 140 stitches ÷ 14
> = a design size of 10 x 10in (25 x 25cm).

When calculating design sizes for evenweave fabrics, divide the fabric count by 2 before you start, because evenweave is worked over two threads not one block as with Aida fabric.

Always add a generous margin when calculating fabric requirements, to allow for finishing and making up. I add 13cm (5in) to both dimensions when stitching a sampler.

Starting and Finishing Stitching

Unless indicated otherwise in the project instructions, begin stitching in the middle of the fabric and the centre of the chart to ensure adequate margins for making up. Start and finish neatly, avoiding knots that cause lumps. Two starting methods are described here.

Knotless loop start This neat start can be used with an even number of strands i.e., 2, 4 or 6. To stitch with two strands, begin with one strand twice the length you'd normally need – about 80cm (30in). Double the thread and thread the needle with the two ends. Put the needle up through the fabric from the wrong side, where you intend to begin stitching, leaving the loop at the back (Fig 1). Form a half cross stitch, put the needle back through the fabric and through the waiting loop. The stitch is now anchored and you may begin.

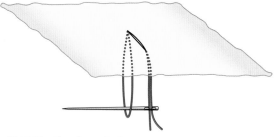

Fig 1 Knotless loop start

Away waste knot start Start this way if using an odd number of strands. Thread your needle with the number of strands required and knot the end. Insert the needle into the right side of the fabric about 2.5cm (1in) away from where you wish to begin stitching (Fig 2). Work your stitching towards the knot and cut it off when the threads are anchored. The alternative is to snip off the knot, thread a needle and work the thread under a few stitches to anchor it.

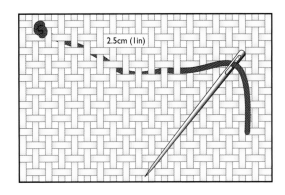

2.5cm (1in)

Fig 2 Away waste knot start

Finishing Stitching

At the back of the work, pass the needle and thread under several stitches of the same or similar colour, and then snip off the loose end close to the stitching. You can begin a new colour in a similar way.

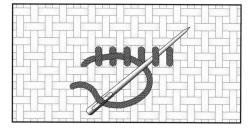

Fig 3 Finishing stitching

Cross Stitching on Evenweave

An evenweave fabric may have thick and thin fibres and quite dramatic slubs in the material. To even out any oddities in the weave, cross stitch is usually worked over two threads of the fabric in each direction. An evenweave can be worked over one thread, for miniature work or when fine detail is required. It is also possible to stitch poems or other text over one thread within a small sampler. If working over one thread, each cross stitch must be completed rather than worked in two journeys because part of the stitch will tend to slip under the fabric threads. When working on evenweave over two fabric threads, start the first cross stitch to the left of a vertical thread (Fig 4). This makes it easier to spot counting mistakes because each stitch will start in the same position relevant to adjacent threads of the fabric.

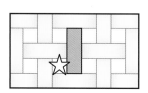

Fig 4 Starting to the left of a vertical thread

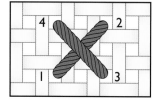

Fig 5 Single cross stitch on evenweave fabric

Cross stitches on evenweave can be formed individually (Fig 5) or in a sewing movement in two journeys, working half cross stitches along a row and completing the crosses on the return journey (Fig 6). This quicker method forms neat single vertical lines on the back, which give somewhere to finish raw ends.

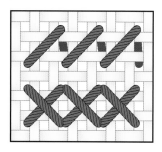

Fig 6 Cross stitch worked in two journeys on evenweave

Cross Stitching on Aida

When stitching on Aida, one block on the fabric corresponds to one square on a chart and cross stitch is usually worked over one block. To work a single cross stitch, bring the needle up from the wrong side of the fabric at the bottom left of a block. Cross one block diagonally and insert the needle into the top right corner (Fig 7). Come up at the bottom right corner and cross to the top left to complete the stitch. To work an adjacent stitch, bring the needle up at the bottom right corner of the first stitch. Cross stitches on Aida can be worked singly or in two journeys – work half cross stitches along a row and then complete the cross stitches on the return journey (shown in Fig 6 for evenweave). Whichever way you choose, for a neat effect, make sure the top stitches all face in the same direction.

Fig 7 Single cross stitch on Aida fabric

Three-Quarter Cross Stitch

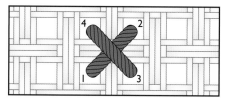

Three-quarter cross stitch is a fractional stitch that produces the illusion of curves. The stitch can be formed on Aida or evenweave but is more successful on evenweave, as the formation of the stitch leaves a hole for the quarter stitch.

Work the first half of the cross stitch as usual, sloping the stitch in the direction shown on the chart you are using (see examples in the corners of the diagram below). Always work the second 'quarter' stitch over the top and down into the central hole to anchor the first half of the stitch. If using Aida, push the needle through the centre of a block of the fabric. Where two three-quarter stitches lie back to back in the space of a full cross stitch, work both of the respective 'quarter' stitches into the central hole.

Fig 8 Three-quarter cross stitch on evenweave

Stitch Perfect Tips

These tried and tested tips have been developed over 20 years of enthusiastic cross stitching and seem to cover most eventualities. I hope you find them helpful.

✔ Organize your threads before you start a project, as this will help to avoid problems later. Always include the manufacturer's name and shade number.

✔ Separate the strands on a skein of stranded cotton (floss) then take the number you need and realign them before threading your needle.

✔ Start with the loop method when using two, four or six strands. This method avoids the muddle often found on the wrong side of a piece of embroidery.

✔ Plan your route around the chart, counting over short distances to avoid mistakes.

✔ Work your cross stitch in two directions in a sewing movement – half cross stitch in one direction and then cover those original stitches with the second row. This forms single vertical lines on the back that are very neat and give somewhere to finish raw ends.

✔ Remember that for neatest work the top stitches should all face the same direction.

✔ Avoid coming up through occupied holes from the back (where a stitch has already been formed). Instead, insert the needle from the front, as this will prevent existing stitches being spoilt.

✔ As you stitch you may find that the threads start to corkscrew slightly and spoil the appearance of the stitches. Either turn the work upside-down and allow the needle to spin, or each time you take the needle out of the fabric give it a half turn before you re-insert it and the stitches will then lie flat.

✔ During cross stitch embroidery, remember to count fabric threads rather than the holes and you will be less likely to make counting errors.

✔ If you are adding a backstitch outline, always add it after the cross stitch has been completed to prevent the solid line of the backstitch being broken. Work the stitches over each block, resisting the temptation to use longer stitches as this will show!

House Samplers

A little girl called Ann Passmore worked the house sampler shown above using wools on canvas, dating and signing her work. The traditional image of a sampler with alphabets, featuring a house with trees, signed and dated by the child is the most familiar image evoked by the word 'sampler'.

During the late 18th to early 19th century, the tradition of sampler making was commonly seen in schools, orphanages and latterly in the workhouses of Victorian Britain. Generally the elements included an upper and lower case alphabet, a house and stylized tree motifs and a counted border pattern. Examples of school samplers can sometimes be identified by how the building was stitched, by the use of certain motifs and so on. I've created my own unique sampler design, opposite, combining hedgerow flowers with a colourful alphabet. Most importantly, the house and garden are the central feature.

Wild Hedgerow House Sampler

I wanted to create a sampler that had a historic feel to it but using modern materials so I have used unbleached 25-count linen and stranded cottons (floss) rather than canvas and wools. You could also work the design on a 14-count Aida. Most of the design is worked in pure cross stitch with no fractional stitches, although I have introduced a few additional counted stitches to the garden area in the foreground. When designing the border for my house sampler I wanted to move away from the formal symmetrical border and create something fuller and wilder and, frankly, more fun to stitch.

Wild Hedgerow House Sampler

Stitch count 198 x 182
Design size 38.5 x 35.5cm (15¼ x 14in)

Create Your Own …

SAMPLER HOUSE

It's easy to personalize the house on this sampler. Draw a box on graph paper using the same number of squares as in the main sampler. Experiment sketching roof shapes and window sizes. When drawing houses for traditional samplers, keep the outline simple, showing a front view of the house, drawn in a rather childlike fashion. Details can be added as you stitch.

If you have charting software this is a chance to use it. When you have sketched the outline of the house, transfer this in backstitch on to the screen. Now try different window and door shapes, using the copy and paste facility to repeat as required. Use the colour palette to add the shades to the outline. If charting your own house, take a shade card outside and look at the walls – you might be surprised at the colours you find. When adding colour to the body of the house, try darker shades (one shade apart perhaps) under the windows, just under the roof and near the ground to add a sense of perspective.

1 Fold the fabric in four and mark the folds with tacking (basting) stitches. Oversew or hem the raw edges of the fabric to prevent fraying. Starting at the centre of the chart and fabric and using a loop start (page 11), follow the chart on pages 18–21. Refer to the Stitch Library for working the stitches.

2 Work the full and three-quarter cross stitch first over two linen threads (or one Aida block) using two strands of stranded cotton (floss) and keeping the top stitches facing in the same direction. Use one strand for the backstitch in the shades indicated on the chart. Use an

away waste knot start (page 11) with one strand of each colour in the needle to work the tweeded stitches on the roofs of the houses.

3 To work the queen stitches and Algerian eyes, stitch over four fabric threads with two strands of stranded cotton (floss). Work half Rhodes stitch over six threads with two strands. Use two strands for the satin stitch, eyelets and French knots, following the positions and colours on the chart.

4 When stitching is complete, check for missed stitches, remove tacking (basting) and mount and frame as preferred (see page 100). Wadding (batting) has been used to give the work an attractive padded look.

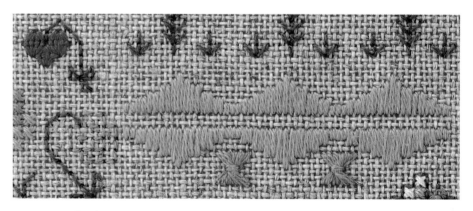

Stitching detail showing queen stitch (far top left), satin stitch (centre) and two half Rhodes stitches (bottom).

Hedgerow Heart Sachet

Stitch this charming heart-shaped sachet for a weekend project. It uses some of the lovely motifs in the main sampler, recombined to create a pleasingly symmetrical design and charted on page 98. You could fill the sachet with scented pot-pourri when making up.

Stitch count 73 x 85   **Design size** 13.25 x 15.5cm (5¼ x 6in)
You will need 31 x 25cm (12 x 10in) buttermilk 28-count Zweigart Cashel linen (or 14-count Aida) • 31 x 25cm (12 x 10in) silk moiré fabric • polyester stuffing • narrow ribbon for a hanging loop

Fold the fabric in four and mark the folds with tacking (basting) stitches. Start stitching from the centre of the chart and the centre of the fabric, using a loop start (page 11) and working over two linen threads (or one Aida block). Work cross stitch using two strands of stranded cotton (floss) and backstitch with one strand. Remove tacking when stitching is complete.

To make up the heart, copy the heart shape given on page 103 on to paper. Use this template to cut a piece of silk moiré. Trim your embroidered fabric to this shape, making sure the stitching is centred in the heart shape. With right sides facing, machine the two pieces together leaving a gap at the top for turning. Turn right side out and press on the back. Stuff the shape quite firmly with polyester stuffing and pot-pourri if you wish. Tuck a doubled piece of narrow ribbon for a hanging loop into the gap and slipstitch closed.

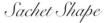

Sachet Shape

Make a sachet of any shape by choosing motifs and borders from the main sampler and creating your own design to fit.

Butterfly House Sampler

This delightful little sampler makes a feature of the tiny butterflies that flit throughout the main sampler. Simple-to-work eyelet stitches provide additional interest. This mini sampler is worked on linen Aida (see page 10) and is charted on page 99.

Stitch count 78 x 96   **Design size** 14 x 17.5cm (5½ x 6¾in)
You will need 30.5 x 25cm (12 x 10in) 14-count linen Aida

Fold the fabric in four and mark the folds with tacking (basting) stitches. Start stitching from the centre of the chart and the centre of the fabric, using a loop start (page 11) and working over one block. Work cross stitches and eyelet stitches using two strands of stranded cotton (floss) and backstitch with one strand.

When stitching is complete, check for missed stitches, remove tacking (basting) and mount and frame as preferred (see page 100).

DMC (ANCHOR)

Cross stitch

⊠⊠	316	(1017)	✦✦	552	(100)	⊞⊞	823	(127)
✱✱	351	(10)	✖✖	554	(90)	GG	840	(903)
⊖⊖	352	(9)	YY	676	(891)	AA	920	(1004)
○○	353	(8)	△△	677	(886)	++	931	(1034)
TT	402	(1047)	◐◐	721	(324)	BB	932	(920)
✕✕	470	(267)	PP	722	(323)	◼◼	937	(268)
VV	471	(265)	SS	725	(298)	==	3042	(870)
LL	472	(253)	⁄⁄	729	(890)	▨▨	3350	(63)

French knots

NN	3740	(872)	
�‒➒	3772	(379)	
NN	blanc	(2)	
++	407 + 840		
	(914 + 903)		
	tweeded together		

Additional backstitch
colours needed:

550 (101)
317 (400)

🌀	729	(890)
●	840	(903)
🌀	931	(1034)
🌀	407 + 840	
	(914 + 903)	
	tweeded together	

Special stitches

🌟 Algerian eye in 351 (10)

◈ Queen stitch in 3350 (63)

▦ Satin stitch in 471 (265)

✸ Half Rhodes in 351 (10)

✳ Eyelet in 729 (890)

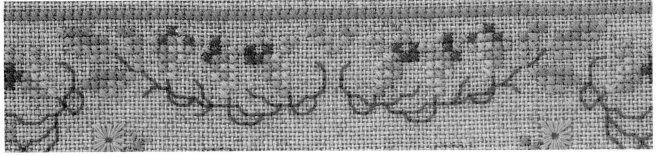

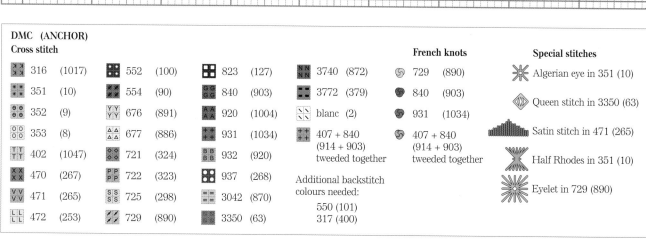

DMC (ANCHOR)

Cross stitch

316	(1017)	552	(100)	823	(127)			
351	(10)	554	(90)	840	(903)			
352	(9)	676	(891)	920	(1004)			
353	(8)	677	(886)	931	(1034)			
402	(1047)	721	(324)	932	(920)			
470	(267)	722	(323)	937	(268)			
471	(265)	725	(298)	3042	(870)			
472	(253)	729	(890)	3350	(63)			

French knots

3740	(872)	
3772	(379)	
blanc	(2)	
407 + 840 (914 + 903) tweeded together		

729	(890)	
840	(903)	
931	(1034)	
407 + 840 (914 + 903) tweeded together		

Additional backstitch colours needed:

550 (101)
317 (400)

Special stitches

Algerian eye in 351 (10)

Queen stitch in 3350 (63)

Satin stitch in 471 (265)

Half Rhodes in 351 (10)

Eyelet in 729 (890)

Links to the Past

In English schools during the Victorian period, it was quite common for 60 children as young as eight years of age to be working on their samplers at any one time, possibly sharing the same school pattern. Now highly collectable, these house samplers are a charming illustration of times gone by, and a reminder of the patience and endeavour of Victorian children.

Alphabet Samplers
ABC

With the exception of house samplers, alphabet samplers are one of the most well-known styles of sampler. They were often a first attempt at counted cross stitch because the lettering is generally simple and could be personalized. Alphabets were stitched on school samplers as well as when training girls for household service, as such skills were needed when marking laundry and caring for household linens.

I have collected a number of alphabet samplers, some plain, others very decorative. I bought the Baird sampler (above) as one of a trio stitched by the same family around 1800. One sampler in the trio is incomplete and I often wonder what happened to the third girl. The Baird sampler combines the use of decorative lettering with a less formal but elegant border, an idea I have used in my own design. In creating my own alphabet sampler, my aim was to include many different styles of alphabet but also to get a flavour of the Baird sampler by working a lush decorative border.

Fanciful Flowers Alphabet Sampler

For my sampler, I was partly inspired by the flowers in my sampler collection and by work seen at exhibitions. I realized that earlier samplers, particularly from the 18th century, did not always have repeating borders and had seen a number with flowers 'growing' up the fabric, so I tried to capture that idea. The vase and flowers are from my imagination but they do echo the feel of the samplers I had in mind. I could have added lots of little insects but in the end decided it was busy enough! The alphabets were a selection of types and styles that felt right in the context. I worked my sampler on 28-count linen for authenticity but it could also be worked on 14-count Aida.

Fanciful Flowers Alphabet Sampler

◇◇◇◇◇◇◇◇◇◇◇◇◇◇◇◇◇◇◇◇◇◇◇◇◇

Stitch count 229 x 200
Design size 41.5 x 36.3cm (16¼ x 14¼in)

You will need

56 x 48cm (22 x 19in) ivory
28-count linen (Zweigart shade 224)

Stranded cotton (floss)
as listed in the chart key

Tapestry needle size 24

Create Your Own...

ABC

ALPHABET SAMPLERS

Alphabet samplers are great fun to compile, particularly if you have charting design software as the letters of the alphabet are easy to combine in a variety of shapes, styles and colours. You can mix italic letters and block capitals if you wish, adding some decorative elements if you are left with some awkward spaces to fill. Why not try working some of the letters in Algerian eye stitch or double cross stitch to create a different effect? In order to work out what size your finished sampler will be and choose the correct amount of fabric to work on, see calculating design size on page 11.

1 Fold the fabric in four and mark the folds with tacking (basting) stitches. Oversew or hem the raw edges of the fabric to prevent fraying. Beginning at the centre of the chart and fabric and using a loop start (page 11), follow the chart on pages 26–29.

2 Work over two linen threads (or one Aida block) using two strands of stranded cotton (floss) for full and three-quarter cross stitches, keeping the top stitch facing the same direction. Use two strands for French knots in the quotation and one strand for the backstitch, using the shades given on the chart.

3 I have added some simple words in the garland at the bottom of the

All things bright and beautiful.

border but feel free to add your own words, or date and sign the sampler in this space – see page 98 for a charted backstitch alphabet.

4 When stitching is complete, check for missed stitches, remove tacking (basting) and mount and frame as preferred (see page 100). Wadding (batting) has been used to give the sampler an attractive padded look.

Personalizing Designs

If adding names and dates to samplers or stitching your own messages, it is best to plan the lettering out on graph paper first, to ensure it fits the space available.

Flowers Needle Fold

Using part of the border motif from the chart on page 29, I have created a pretty needle fold, which has a folded hem and is lined with blue felt. I have added some needle types in backstitch, which helps to keep my gold-plated needles in order (see picture top of opposite page). This project needs to be worked on linen if you intend to work the folded hem.

Stitch count 71 x 46 flower vase motif
Design size 12.5 x 8.25cm (5 x 3¼in)
You will need 35.5 x 18cm (14 x 7in) light stone 25-count Dublin linen (Zweigart shade 52) • dark blue felt • a small button for fastening

Work the needle fold design in the centre of the fabric, using two strands of stranded cotton (floss) for cross stitch and one strand for backstitch.

Count four fabric threads from the top and bottom of the stitching and work a row of four-sided stitch over four fabric threads, using two strands of cream. Steam press the embroidery with some spray starch prior to working the hemstitch.

Work the hemstitch by first measuring 7cm (2¾in) from the four-sided stitch towards the raw edge and removing one fabric thread. Do the same at the other end of the stitching. On each long side, count four threads outwards from the stitching and remove one fabric thread. Work a folded hem around the whole design (see page 93 for stitching a folded hem), checking that when the flaps are folded to the back they meet in the middle. If desired, add the backstitch writing to the needle fold as shown in the picture below – see page 98 for a charted backstitch alphabet.

Lay the hemmed stitching right side down and cut a piece of felt as a lining. Using a sharp needle, hemstitch the felt inside the project, re-using the holes made when the hemstitch

was first worked. On the right side, using dark blue thread, work one row of counted chain stitch using the hemstitch holes. To fasten the needle fold, add a pretty button and a button loop (see page 89).

Stitcher's Nécessaire

I have used the lovely vase and flower motif on the front of this simple sewing roll formerly known as a nécessaire or hussif, which is a case with pockets for small tools and certainly useful for keeping pins, scissors and a few needles. The design can be worked on linen or Aida.

Stitch count 120 x 46   **Design size** 21 x 8.25cm (8½ x 3¼in)
You will need 30.5 x 15cm (12 x 6in) beige 28-count Perleinen (Zweigart shade 53) • beige 32-count Belfast linen (shade 345) for pockets • polyester wadding (batting) • dark blue lining fabric • bias binding (bought or homemade)

Work the design in the centre of the fabric, using two strands of stranded cotton (floss) for cross stitch and one for backstitch. You could also add some flower motifs to the pockets faces prior to making up, as shown here.

To make up the nécessaire, cut a curve to the top of the stitching – a small plate will help achieve this rounded shape. Using the embroidery as a template cut lining fabric and polyester wadding (batting) to match.

To make the two pockets, cut two pieces of linen 15 x 9cm (6 x 3½in) and bind one straight edge on each pocket (see making bias binding page 101). Lay the pocket sections on the lining, right sides together.

Stitch the pocket to the lining with one straight seam each, so that once pressed you can turn the pocket upwards and tack (baste) in position, thus hiding the straight seam.

Now sandwich the cross stitch, wadding (batting) and linen lining together, right sides out and pin carefully. Ideally, zigzag around the edge of the whole project and trim away excess fabric.

Bind the short straight edge with bias binding. Attaching bias binding around the rest of the nécessaire will neaten the edges and also complete the pockets. To attach binding, either machine first on the wrong side and then top stitch down on the right side, or vice versa.

DMC (ANCHOR)

Cross stitch

P P P 223 (10)	L L L 472 (293)	H H H 738 (880)	3012 (365)
+ + 224 (1021)	Y Y Y 676 (301)	930 (1036)	3740 (972)
▲ ▲ 316 (76)	712 (2)	B B 931 (978)	3013 (278)
▽ ▽ 437 (891)	729 (306)	X X 3011 (277)	3041 (1027)
			V V 3721 (29)

3740 (972)
3752 (1037)
3777 (20)

French knots

3011 (277)

3011

Links to the Past

Wondering about the stories that samplers could tell us
about people of past eras is one of the fascinating aspects of studying
antique samplers. I can still remember a visit in the early 1990s to an exhibition at the
Metropolitan Museum in Los Angeles, USA, where the antique alphabet samplers were so
beautifully stitched that I did not pick up a needle for weeks! One of the samplers, worked
by a twelve-year-old girl, had been stitched by moonlight
and I often imagine what her life was like.

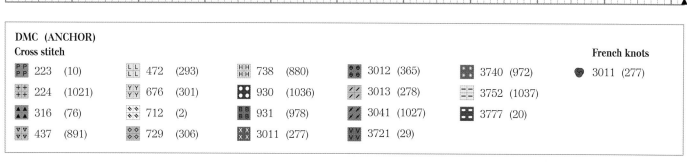

3011

3777

930

3777

3011

3011

French knot
in 3011

3011

3011

3011

All t

bright and

DMC (ANCHOR)

Cross stitch

					French knots
P P P / 223 (10)	L L L / 472 (293)	H H H / 738 (880)	3012 (365)	3740 (972)	3011 (277)
+ + + / 224 (1021)	Y Y Y / 676 (301)	930 (1036)	3013 (278)	3752 (1037)	
▲▲ / 316 (76)	712 (2)	B B B / 931 (978)	3041 (1027)	3777 (20)	
▽▽ / 437 (891)	729 (306)	X X X / 3011 (277)	V V V / 3721 (29)		

3011

3777

3011

rings

l beautiful,

Map Samplers

Map samplers were commonly worked in educational establishments, like charity schools, orphanages and in more affluent schools as a method of teaching geography, spelling and diligence. As well as country maps, children worked county maps, village plans and designs based on a local farm or estate.

The map of Europe above is one of the finest samplers in my collection and another antique-fair find. The dealer wasn't really interested in textiles and didn't push the price too high. I was thrilled to find that all the names, longitude and latitude and the border were worked in tiny stitches on linen. It was, however, worked on a pre-printed fabric rather than being a counted example. Another charming element of map samplers are the ships, sea monsters and mythical creatures that often fill the oceans – always an inspiration to a stitcher and an idea I have used in my map sampler, opposite.

Map of England Sampler

This sampler started life some years ago when my husband kept nagging me to design a sampler based on the old 'real' counties of England. In the end I suggested that he went away and design it himself! The map part of this sampler is his creation and I have added the very decorative border to echo the map samplers in my collection. I have a number of maps, all in various stages of disrepair, all with different borders and decorative motifs. I love the little boats and sea monsters that are often seen in antique maps both stitched and as old prints. My sampler was worked on 28-count linen but it could also be worked on 14-count Aida.

Map of England Sampler

◇◇◇◇◇◇◇◇◇◇◇◇◇◇◇◇◇◇

Stitch count 219 x 196
Design size 40 x 35.5cm (15½ x 14in)

You will need

53 x 48cm (21 x 19in) ivory
28-count Cashel linen
(Zweigart shade 224)

Stranded cotton (floss)
as listed in chart key

Tapestry needle size 24

Create Your Own ...

MAP SAMPLER

Maps are a fascinating source of
material for stitchers and non-stitchers
alike. I know from personal experience
that even non-stitching men like to
mess with maps. Using tracing paper,
pencil and eraser, my husband charted
my first cross stitch map kit over 20
years ago. You need to start with a good
outline of the area you intend to chart
and remember to keep the chart simple
– details can be added as you stitch.
I have charted and stitched a map of the
United States of America (shown right)
using the same border and ship motifs
as the English map. There isn't enough
room to include the chart here but it can
be obtained from The Cross Stitch Guild
(see Suppliers page 104).

1 Fold the fabric in four and mark the
folds with tacking (basting) stitches.
Oversew or hem the raw edges of the
fabric to prevent fraying.
Beginning at the
centre of the chart
and fabric and
using a loop
start (page 11),
follow the chart
on pages 34–37.

2 Work over two linen
threads (or one Aida block) using
two strands of stranded cotton (floss) for
full and three-quarter cross stitches, and
keeping the top stitch facing the same
direction. In order to keep your place

on the chart you may find it helpful
to backstitch the county names as you
complete each one. Use one strand only
for the backstitch in the
counties using the shade
given on the chart.
Use two strands for
the backstitch for
Scotland, Wales and
the sea names.

3 When the stitching
is complete, check
for missed stitches, remove tacking
(basting) and mount and frame as
preferred (see page 100). Wadding
(batting) was used to give the sampler a
nice padded look.

Map of the USA sampler – chart available from The Cross Stitch Guild (see page 104).

Flower Heart Card

This pretty motif has been adapted from the main chart (see chart below). The stitching has been frayed and applied to the card as a patch trimmed with pink ribbon. The design could be worked on linen or Aida.

Stitch count 30 x 43 **Design size** 5.5 x 8cm (2¼ x 3in)
You will need 12.5 x 15.25cm (5 x 6in) candy pink
28-count Cashel linen (Zweigart shade 443)
• single-fold card • decorative paper • craft glue
• double-sided adhesive tape • ribbon to trim

Using a loop start (page 11), work from the centre of the chart and fabric over two linen threads (or one Aida block) using two strands of stranded cotton (floss) for cross stitch and one for backstitch.

Using craft glue, cover the front of the card with decorative paper. Trim the fabric to within 2.5cm (1in) of the embroidery all round, fray the edges and fix the patch to the card with double-sided tape. Trim with pretty ribbon as desired.

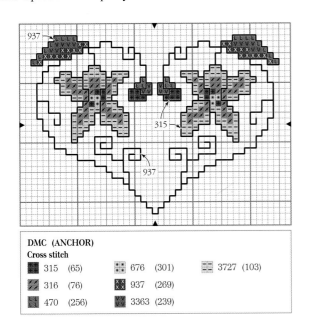

DMC (ANCHOR)
Cross stitch

◼	315	(65)	▦	676	(301)	▨	3727 (103)
◪	316	(76)	✖	937	(269)		
◩	470	(256)	ⱽ	3363	(239)		

Traveller's Tales Card

For this attractive card I have used a ship from the map sampler, repeating and adapting it and adding some text (see chart below). The card is made using decorative paper and plain card. The design could also be worked on Aida.

Stitch count 19 x 41 **Design size** 3.5 x 7.5cm (1¼ x 3in)
You will need 12.5 x 15.25cm (5 x 6in) tea-dyed 28-count Cashel Vintage linen (Zweigart shade 3009) • single-fold card • decorative paper • craft glue • double-sided adhesive tape

Using a loop start (page 11), work from the centre of the chart and fabric. Work over two linen threads (or one block of Aida) using two strands of stranded cotton (floss) for full and three-quarter cross stitch and one strand for backstitch.

Using craft glue, cover the front of the card with decorative paper. Trim the fabric to within 2.5cm (1in) of the embroidery all round, fray the edges and fix the patch to the card with double-sided tape.

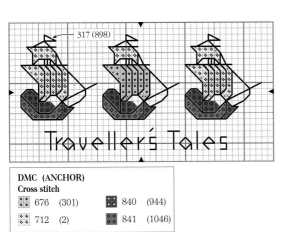

DMC (ANCHOR)
Cross stitch

▦	676	(301)	◆	840	(944)
▥	712	(2)	▨	841	(1046)

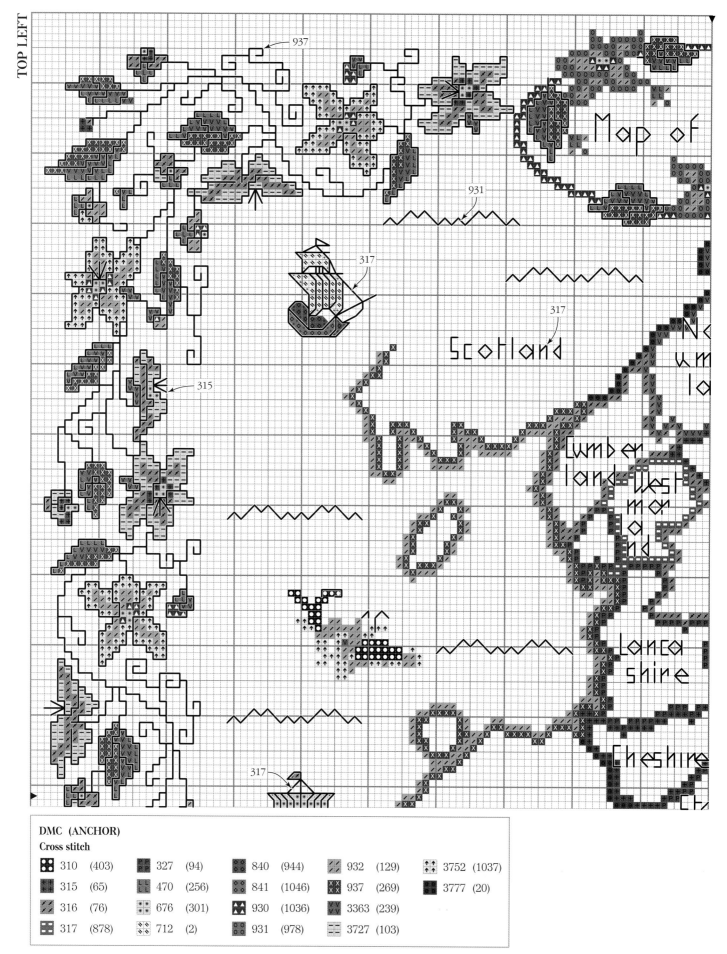

Map of

Scotland

931

937

317

315

317

317

Nо
vm
la

Cumber
land West
mor
la
nd

Lanca
shire

Cheshire

317

DMC (ANCHOR)
Cross stitch

310	(403)	327	(94)	840	(944)	932	(129)	3752	(1037)
315	(65)	470	(256)	841	(1046)	937	(269)	3777	(20)
316	(76)	676	(301)	930	(1036)	3363	(239)		
317	(878)	712	(2)	931	(978)	3727	(103)		

315

930

England

930

931

The
North
Sea

930

930

930

N

930

937

937

orth
iber
ind

315

315

315

Durham

937

937

317

Yorkshire

317

930

Derby Nott Lincoln
shire ing shire
ham

315

Links to the Past

I have a few map samplers, all slightly different –
some counted, some on pre-printed fabrics. The counted ones
are particularly charming, with the child's home town and
nearby villages marked but major cities like London left out
altogether. One can imagine that, when the world was a
smaller place, if you lived in the York area, you
would know of local towns but have little knowledge
of the rest of the country.

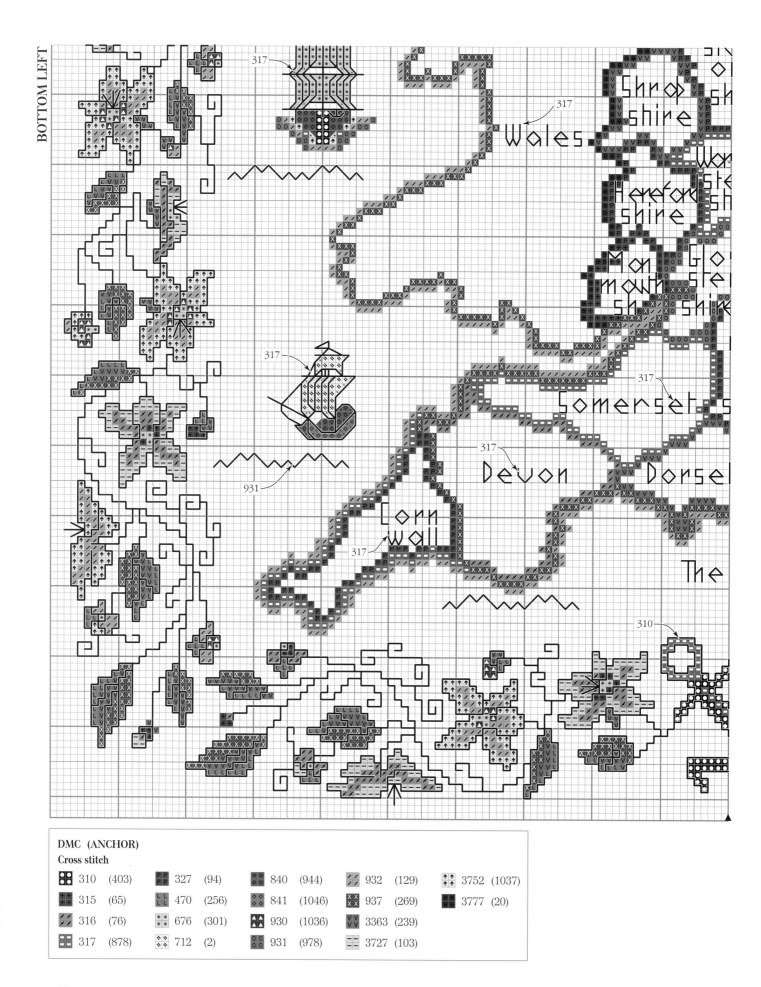

DMC (ANCHOR)

Cross stitch

310 (403)	327 (94)	840 (944)	932 (129)	3752 (1037)
315 (65)	470 (256)	841 (1046)	937 (269)	3777 (20)
316 (76)	676 (301)	930 (1036)	3363 (239)	
317 (878)	712 (2)	931 (978)	3727 (103)	

Leicester
shire
Norfolk
Com
War
North
bri
ice wick
amp
Hunts
shire
tonsh
Bed
sh
Suffolk
ford
Buck
sh
hent
317
Oxford
ire
sh
Essex
sh
ham sh
Berk
Midd
shire
Lon don
Wilt
shire
Kent
Hamp
Surrey
shire
317
Sussex
317
931
English Channel
930

937
937
930
930
310
315
930

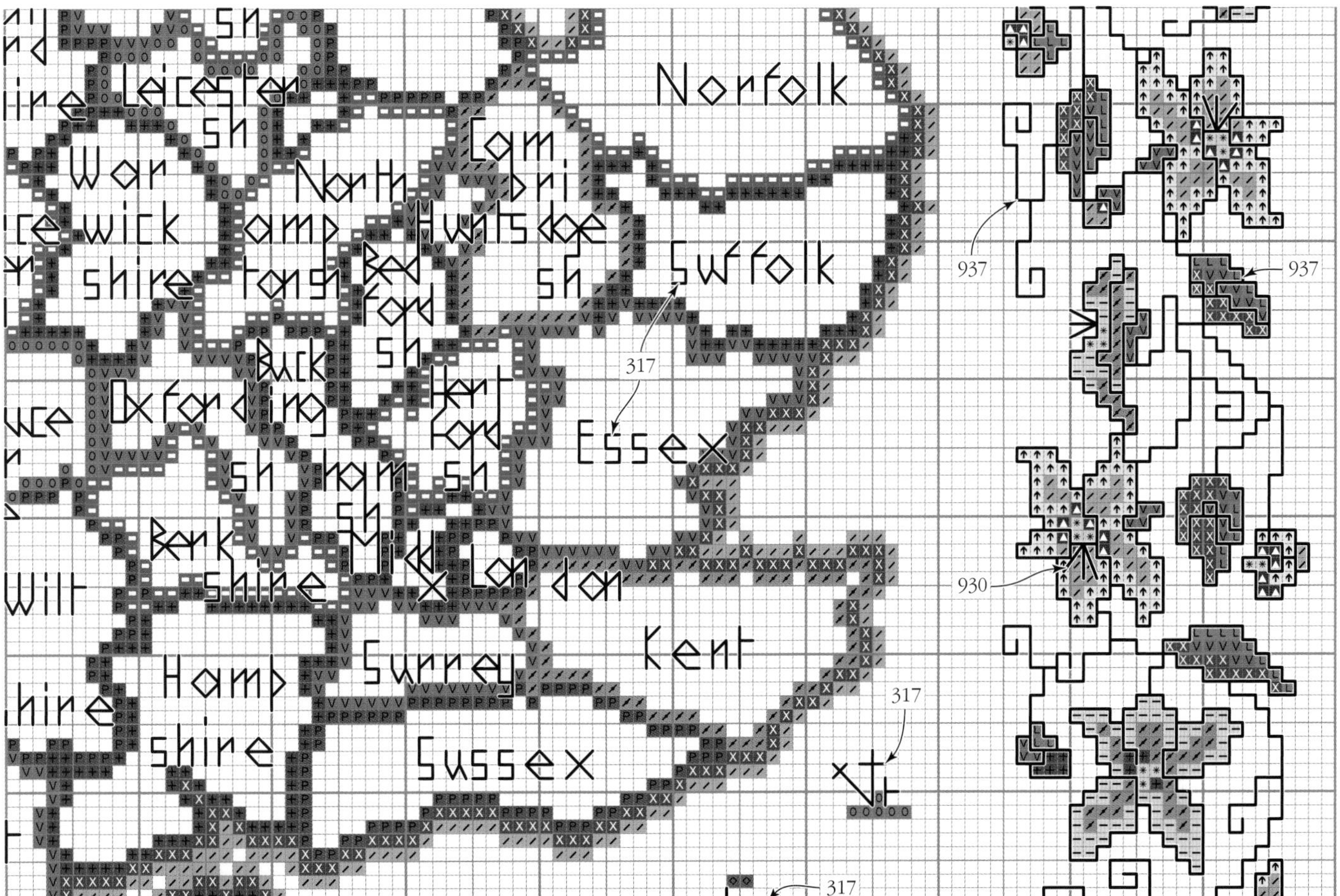

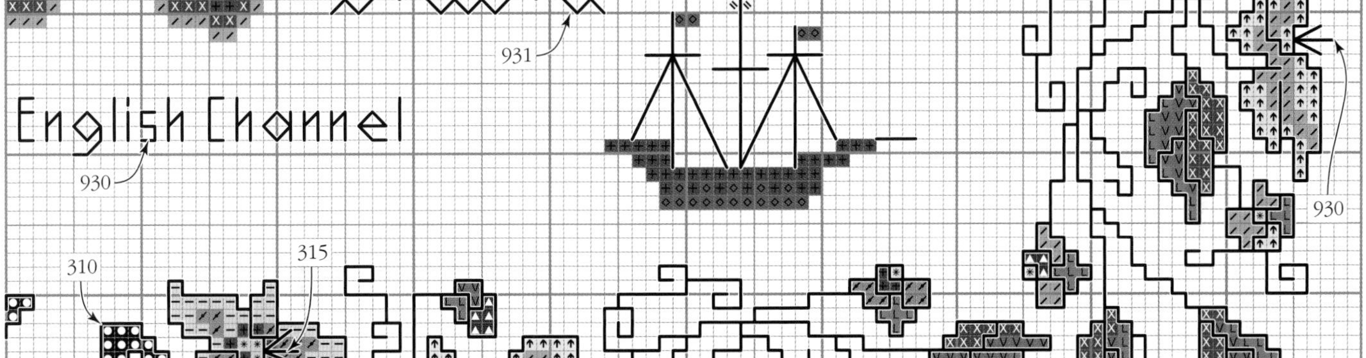

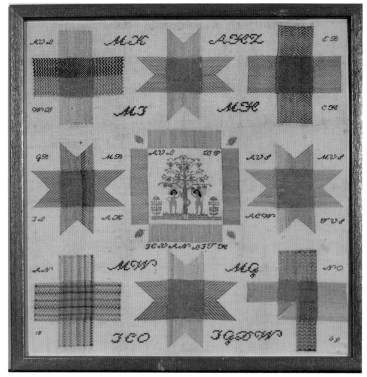

Darning Samplers

The very idea of darning, particularly darning socks, leaves me cold but pattern darning for fun is so satisfying. Over the past years, I have found two darning samplers to add to my collection. Surviving examples are generally dated 1770–1820 and are found in the UK, Germany, Holland and Denmark.

The Adam and Eve darning sampler (above) was stitched in Germany, probably in an orphanage by the children. Each darning pattern was stitched by a different group of children using the most delicate and tiny stitches imaginable and then signed with their initials. It is worked on very fine linen and in some cases worked over one thread of the fabric. I bought the sampler from an avid textile collector whilst visiting a trade fair in Germany. I was quite unable to resist the charming Adam and Eve motif in the centre and all the gorgeous patterns, some of which feature in my own darning sampler.

Gardenia Darning Sampler

Darning samplers vary enormously in their character and decorative elements, so my version (shown right) is really a combination of designs I have seen and patterns from my own collection. I have used a flower outline that could be used as a cross stitch or blackwork pattern (see the band sampler on page 80 for ideas) or filled with darning patterns. You can follow my version or work the backstitch outline of the flower and fill the petals with your own patterns. During stitching I found that once a few rows of the pattern were in place I no longer needed the chart because you can see where you are supposed to be. The sampler can really only be worked on linen as some of the patterns are worked over one fabric thread.

Gardenia Darning Sampler

◇◇◇◇◇◇◇◇◇◇◇◇◇◇◇◇◇◇◇◇◇

Stitch count 162 x 155
Design size 30 x 28cm (11½ x 11in)

Create Your Own ...

DARNING PATTERNS

As you can see from the small projects on the opposite page, pattern darns are very attractive in their own right and make excellent decorations for small items. You could experiment with a few of the patterns supplied in the main chart on pages 42–45 using different colourways. If you want to create a more complex project, why not select an outline of a flower or an abstract pattern of a little house shape and fill this with different darning patterns? It is a good idea to start the pattern in the centre of a designated area and then allow the pattern to fill the space.

To create your own darning patterns treat yourself to some large-squared graph paper so you can draw lines using coloured crayons. The large squares will enable you to draw lines on the lines and also in the spaces. If you are using computer charting software you can really let yourself go by using any existing cross stitch patterns and, after deleting the cross stitch, filling in the voids with your own choice of coloured pattern darning.

1 Fold the fabric in four and mark the folds with tacking (basting) stitches. Oversew or hem the raw edges of the fabric to prevent fraying. You may find using an embroidery frame helpful as the stitches are worked over different numbers of fabric threads.

2 Using a loop start (page 11) and following the chart on pages 42–45, work over two linen threads, beginning with the gardenia outline in backstitch (or Holbein stitch) using two strands of stranded cotton (floss). To check your position as you stitch, work each petal outline completely, making sure you are returning to the correct place every time. Add the cross stitch stem to the flower, using two strands and working over two linen threads.

3 Using one strand, start to work the darning patterns in the flower, a petal at a time, working in straight rows of running stitch (not backstitch). Once the flower is finished, work the rest of the darning patterns in a similar way, working over the fabric threads indicated on the chart.

4 Finally, work the border using two strands for full and three-quarter cross stitch and one for backstitch.

5 When the stitching is complete, remove tacking (basting) and mount and frame as preferred (see page 100). Alternatively, create a hemstitched edge as described on page 93.

Using Darning Patterns for Cards

Darning patterns are perfect for decorating cards, especially if you like to create your own cards as I do. Since the growth in paper crafts and rubber stamping you can buy the most beautiful handmade papers and cards so have a go at creating your own. I keep a box of useful ribbons, decorative papers and even buttons handy just in case. Once stitched, the darning patterns can be mounted in an aperture card or fixed as a patch to the front of a card (see page 101).

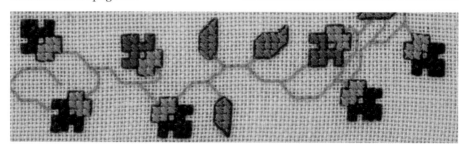

Decorative Darn Bookmark

This bookmark uses a darning pattern from the main sampler, which was then hemstitched and stuck to plain card. For a finishing touch add two decorative buttons and a twisted cord (see page 101). The design can only be worked on linen.

Stitch count 13 x 39   **Design size** 2.5 x 7cm (1 x 2¾in)
You will need 5 x 18cm (2 x 7in) antique white 25-count Dublin linen (Zweigart shade 101) • plain card • two decorative buttons
• double-sided adhesive tape • twisted cord

Using one strand of stranded cotton (floss), work the darning patterns in straight rows of running stitch using the chart on page 44 and extending the pattern by two zigzags.

When complete, press on the wrong side using spray starch and hemstitch the edge. Cut card slightly larger than the embroidery and trim the embroidery to the hemstitched line (see diagram) and stick it to the card

using double-sided tape. Sew some thread through the button holes and stick them to the bookmark, adding twisted cord.

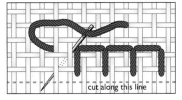

cut along this line

Decorative Darn Coaster

This pretty coaster features one of the darning patterns from the main sampler. The embroidery was trimmed and the edges frayed up to a simple interlaced border. The design needs to be worked on linen.

Stitch count 41 x 42 **Design size** 8.25 x 8.25cm (3¼ x 3¼in)
You will need 15 x 15cm (6 x 6in) antique white 25-count Dublin linen (Zweigart shade 101)

Using one strand of stranded cotton (floss), start to work the darning patterns in straight rows of running stitch, changing colours as shown on the chart on page 44.

When complete, press on the wrong side using spray starch. Create the interlaced border by counting four fabric threads from the stitching and removing two threads. Repeat on all sides. Using a large needle and all six strands of blue stranded cotton (floss), weave the thread under and over three fabric threads, overlapping at the corners as shown. Work a row of white backstitch invisibly outside this blue border to prevent further fraying, then trim the edge and fray to within four threads of the blue border.

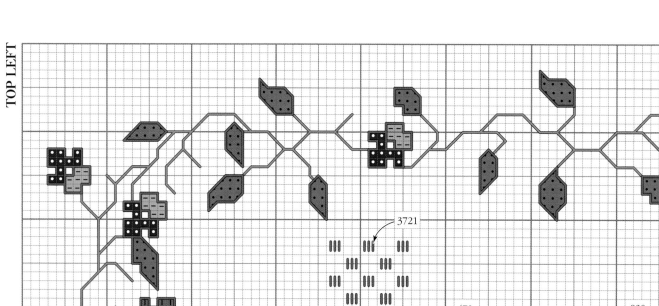

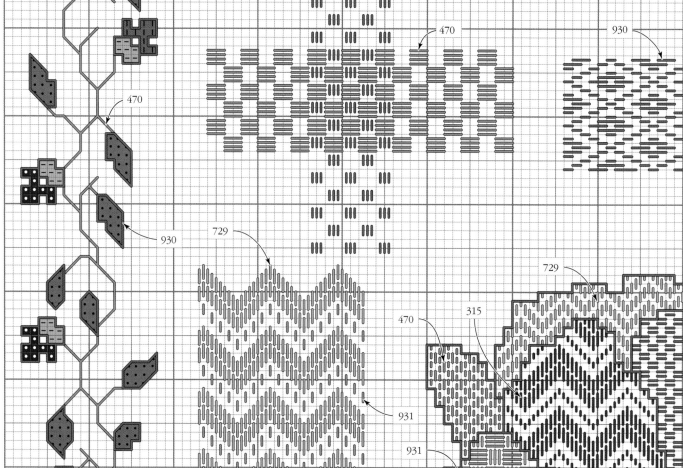

DMC (ANCHOR)
Cross stitch

Running stitch (backstitch for border)

470 (978)	— 223 (10)	— 729 (1018)	— 3041 (65)
729 (1018)	— 315 (256)	— 930 (1036)	— 3721 (306)
930 (1036)	— 470 (978)	— 931 (29)	— 3830 (39)
931 (29)			

3041

223

3830

3721

470

931

930

729

315

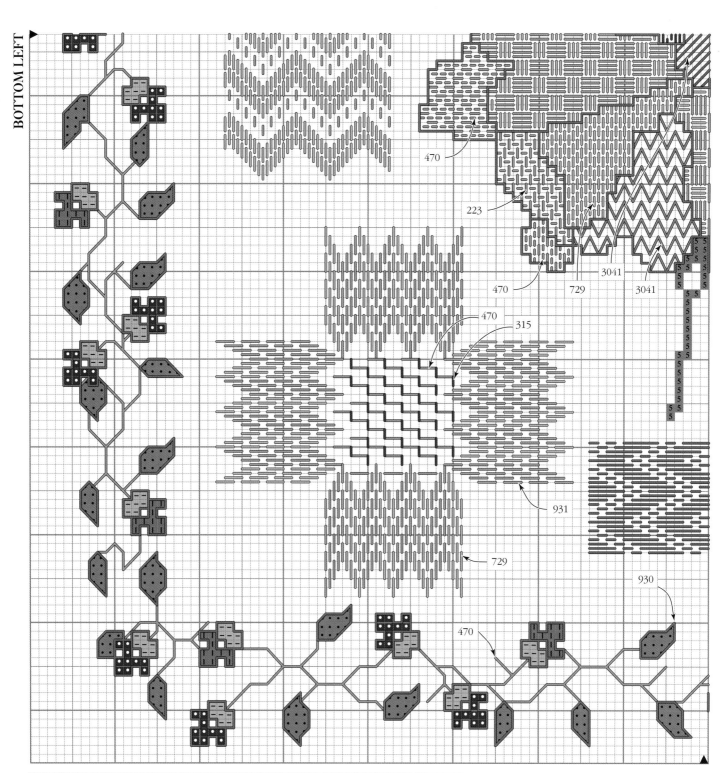

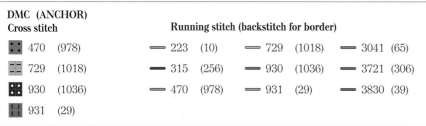

DMC (ANCHOR)
Cross stitch

470 (978)

729 (1018)

930 (1036)

931 (29)

Running stitch (backstitch for border)

— 223 (10)

— 315 (256)

— 470 (978)

— 729 (1018)

— 930 (1036)

— 931 (29)

— 3041 (65)

— 3721 (306)

— 3830 (39)

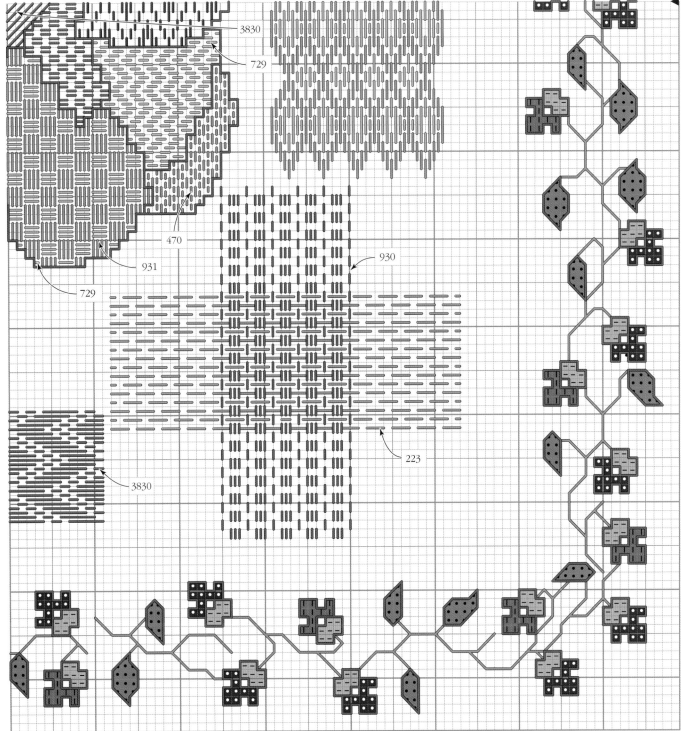

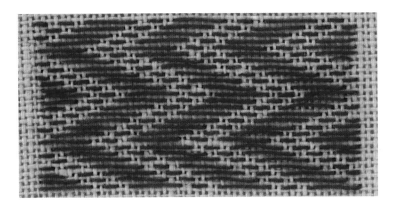

Links to the Past

Our clothes today are much more durable than in earlier times thanks to modern textiles, so darning is not considered a necessary skill. In past times, this skill was valued highly and sampler makers demonstrated this with wonderful pieces of work. I have seen a darning sampler from this period in a gallery priced at £36,000! Having said that, I have seen some remarkable modern darning done by a tailor in the Cotswolds, England, an expert in real pattern darning involving the recreation of tweed.

Spot Motif Samplers

S pot motif samplers were stitched during the 17th century in Britain as a record of stitches and patterns and also for appliqué for garments and furnishings. Many individual designs were stitched on one piece of fabric and rolled and stored in a drawer until more stitching was added.

I'm not lucky enough to own a 17th century motif sampler but do have some antique samplers covered in random patterns. Sarah Hubbard's pretty sampler (above) has all sorts of motifs including birds, animals, trees and flowers. I bought it unframed and with many moth holes, which are now barely visible after some attention. What isn't obvious at first glance is that the design is worked in just reds and greens, proving you do not have to use dozens of colours to create a lovely effect. When Sarah stitched this sampler she hadn't quite mastered the counting and occasionally runs out of fabric: this just adds to the charm and increases my affection for the piece. I have tried to bring this sense of naïve charm to my own spot sampler design.

Garden of Eden Motif Sampler

Inspired by Sarah's intermingling of motifs, I have taken an Adam and Eve motif from one of my antique darning samplers (see picture on page 38) and then added lots of my favourite cross stitch and counted patterns in the same way that a stitcher might have done in the 17th century, although I have worked most of the design in pure cross stitch rather than using many different stitches. I have included a small hemstitch square in the main design and a few additional stitches that must be worked on evenweave rather than Aida. If you prefer you could replace the hemstitch square with a cross stitch motif, perhaps of your own design.

Garden of Eden Motif Sampler

Stitch count 170 x 280
Design size 31 x 51cm (12 x 20in)

You will need

43 x 64cm (17 x 25in) light beige
28-count Cashel linen
(Zweigart shade 345)

Stranded cotton (floss)
as listed in the chart key

Tapestry needle size 24

Create Your Own …

SPOT SAMPLER

For the modern embroiderer, spot
samplers are the perfect answer: just
collect together all your favourite
motifs and then work them all over
the fabric with no attention to subject,
scale or symmetry – pure indulgence!
These types of samplers are the perfect
medium if you want to experiment with
designing for yourself because anything
goes. This process is even easier if
you have cross stitch design software,
because you can cut and paste motifs
to your heart's content; flip them, rotate
them, repeat them – whatever looks
pleasing. You can then choose which
colours work best when you are happy
with the overall shape and balance of
the design.

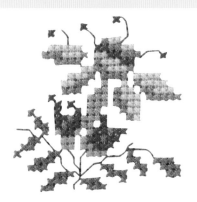

1 Fold the fabric in four and mark the
folds with tacking (basting) stitches.
Oversew or hem the raw edges of the
fabric to prevent fraying. Beginning at
the centre of the chart and fabric and
using a loop start (page 11), follow the
chart on pages 50–53. Refer to the Stitch
Library for working the stitches.

2 Work over two linen threads using
two strands of stranded cotton (floss)
for full and three-quarter cross stitches.
Work queen stitches and French knots
using two strands. Add the backstitch
in one strand, in the colours given on
the chart. If you are not working the
hemstitch square, move on to step 6.

3 **Working a hemstitch square:** using
two strands of cream, work a square
of hemstitch as shown on the chart,
counting each side carefully. As you turn
a corner, count the last stitch on one row
as the first on the next to avoid working
a rectangle! Finish off waste thread.

4 You can now cut the fabric threads.
To ensure that you cut the correct
ones you may find it helpful to run a line
of tacking (basting) threads through the
square as shown in the diagram. Count
to the centre of the hemmed area and
snip alternate pairs. Carefully unravel
the cut threads from the middle to the
hemstitched edge, leaving a two-thread

border at the sides. On the back of the
work, loosely tack (baste) these threads
out of the way – to be dealt with later.

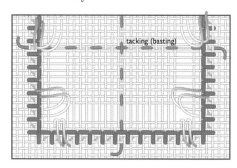

*Above: working the hemstitch square;
below: position of the satin stitch border.*

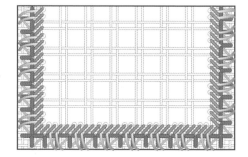

5 To decorate the remaining threads,
wrap each pair with one strand of
cream, adding dove's eye stitches as you
wrap. To complete the square, use two
strands of cream to work one row of
satin stitch around the square. Remove
the tacking and snip off fabric threads.

6 If you are not working the hemstitched square, fill the space with
another motif. The space is about 20 x 20
stitches so try one of the rosebuds from
the Berlin Swallows sampler chart page
66 or a star from the Bristol Orphanage
sampler chart on page 58, changing the
colour as you please. Alternatively, design
your own motif to fit the space.

7 When stitching is complete, remove
tacking (basting) and mount and
frame. Wadding (batting) gives the
sampler a nice padded look.

Ribbon Garland Needle Roll

The cross stitch motif on this pretty needle roll has been taken directly from the main chart on page 50 and is easily made up. The design needs to be stitched on evenweave if you intend to work the hemstitching.

Stitch count 32 x 41
Design size 5.8 x 7.5cm (2¼ x 3in)
You will need 20 x 12.5cm (8 x 5in) pale peach 28-count Cashel linen (Zweigart shade 448) • polyester wadding (batting) • ribbon

Using a loop start (page 11), work from the centre of the charted motif and fabric. Work over two linen threads using two strands of stranded cotton (floss) for cross stitch.

To make up the roll, work a row of hemstitch along the short side using two strands of matching stranded cotton (floss). Trim to the stitching (see diagram on page 41). Fold the long sides together, folding in the raw edges, and slipstitch together to form a tube. Fill the tube with polyester wadding (batting) until fairly firm. Halfway between the cross stitch and the hemstitch, run a line of gathering stitches around the tube, pull tightly to gather and finish off. Tie ribbon around the gathers and trim neatly. Repeat for the other end of the tube.

Flower Vase Picture

This sweet little picture has a pure cross stitch motif taken from the main chart on page 51, which has then been framed diagonally. The design could also be worked on 14-count Aida if you prefer.

Stitch count
49 x 41
Design size
9 x 7.5cm (3½ x 3in)
You will need
18 x 20cm (7 x 8in) candy pink 28-count Cashel linen (Zweigart shade 443)

Using a loop start (page 11), work from the centre of the charted motif and fabric. Cross stitch over two linen threads (or one Aida block) using two strands of stranded cotton (floss).

Check for missed stitches and then mount and frame as preferred (see page 100).

367

367

French knot in 3042

French knot in 930

930

3777

French knots in 729

3777

French knots in 840

840

930

367

349

367

367

DMC (ANCHOR)
Cross stitch

P P P P 223 (10)	L L 470 (256)	↑↑ 743 (289)	■■ 930 (1036)	H H H H 3364 (265)
⊖⊖ ⊖⊖ 224 (1021)	✔✔ 471 (279)	✗✗ 744 (292)	B B B B 931 (978)	➤➤ 3721 (29)
◄◄ 327 (94)	⊞ 632 (245)	C C C C 758 (36)	V V V V 932 (129)	✱✱ 3772 (1049)
R R R R 349 (335)	⋰⋰ 712 (2)	840 (944)	937 (269)	3777 (1005)
✚✚ 350 (333)	▼▼ 729 (306)	◇◇ 926 (208)	‖‖ 951 (926)	
✚✚ 351 (33)				
✱✱ 353 (1020)		■■ 3012 (365)		
✗✗ 367 (245)		➤➤ 3041 (1018)		
⋰⋰ 436 (363)		✱✱ 3042 (390)		
◇◇ 437 (891)		3053 (264)		
		T T 3363 (239)		

French knots

🌀 729 (306)	930 (1036)
● 840 (944)	🌀 3042 (390)

367

930

930

367

367

367

930

840

930

French
knots
in 840

840

632

367

hemstitch square in 712 (2) with
wrapped bars and dove's eyes

632

840

632

930

930

930

367

queen
stitch
in 3777

937

632

367

French knots

729 (306)			
840 (944)			
930 (1036)			
3042 (390)			

DMC (ANCHOR)
Cross stitch

223 (10)	351 (33)	470 (256)	743 (289)	930 (1036)	3012 (365)	HH 3364 (265)
224 (1021)	353 (1020)	471 (279)	744 (292)	931 (978)	3041 (1018)	3721 (29)
327 (94)	367 (245)	632 (20)	758 (36)	932 (129)	3042 (390)	3772 (1049)
349 (335)	436 (363)	712 (2)	840 (944)	937 (269)	3053 (264)	3777 (1005)
350 (333)	437 (891)	729 (306)	926 (208)	951 (926)	3363 (239)	

Red Samplers

The idea of working a sampler in one colour, particularly red, isn't new as they have been popular in France and Germany for years. You can see a fine example of a French sampler worked in red on canvas on page 8 and if you look in needlework shops in Europe, they are still as popular today.

It was when I found this red sampler worked by Catherine Archer (above) that I first heard of the George Müller Foundation and realized that Catherine's sampler had been stitched while she was living at Ashley Down Orphanage, one of the Müller orphanages in Bristol, England (see Links to the Past, page 61). Red samplers are popular in Europe but if you prefer another colour choose one that works with your furnishings and have the background fabric to hand to see how this affects the finished piece. Inspired by Catherine's work, I have charted sections of her sampler for my Bristol Orphanage sampler.

Bristol Orphanage Sampler and Italic Alphabet Cushion

For my alphabet sampler I used one of Catherine's upper case alphabets, one lower case and some repeating border patterns. Catherine worked her design on fabric 40 threads to 2.5cm (1in) and over one thread! My sampler is cross stitched over two threads of 32-count linen – easier on the eye!

The italic alphabet cushion was inspired by the ornate alphabet from the French sampler on page 8. The original was stitched on canvas but I have used traditional unbleached linen. The italic alphabet design would make a great framed picture but for variety I've shown it made up as an inset cushion, with a bright cotton lace trim. Both designs can be worked on linen or Aida fabric.

Bristol Orphanage Sampler

Stitch count 159 x 136
Design size 25.5 x 21.5cm (10 x 8½in)

You will need

38 x 33cm (15 x 13in) cream
32-count Belfast linen
(Zweigart shade 223)

Stranded cotton (floss)
as listed in the chart key

Tapestry needle size 26

1 Fold the fabric in four and mark the folds with tacking (basting) stitches. Using a loop start (page 11), work from the chart overleaf starting at the centre of the chart and fabric.

2 Work all the cross stitch over two linen threads (or one Aida block) using two strands of stranded cotton (floss) for the cross stitch and keeping the top stitch facing the same direction.

3 When the stitching is complete, check for missed stitches, remove tacking (basting) and mount and frame as preferred (see page 100). Wadding (batting) was used to give the picture an attractive padded look.

Create Your Own ...

COLOUR SCHEME

It is easy and fun to stitch an alphabet sampler in a different colour, perhaps to match the furnishings or colour scheme of a particular room. For example, see the little red sampler on the opposite page which has been worked in an attractive blue shade. You will find it useful have the embroidery fabric you plan to use as the background in order to see how this affects the finished piece – for instance, a creamy fabric colour may work better than a bright white if you prefer subtlety over drama.

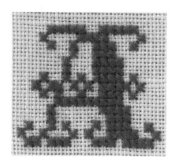

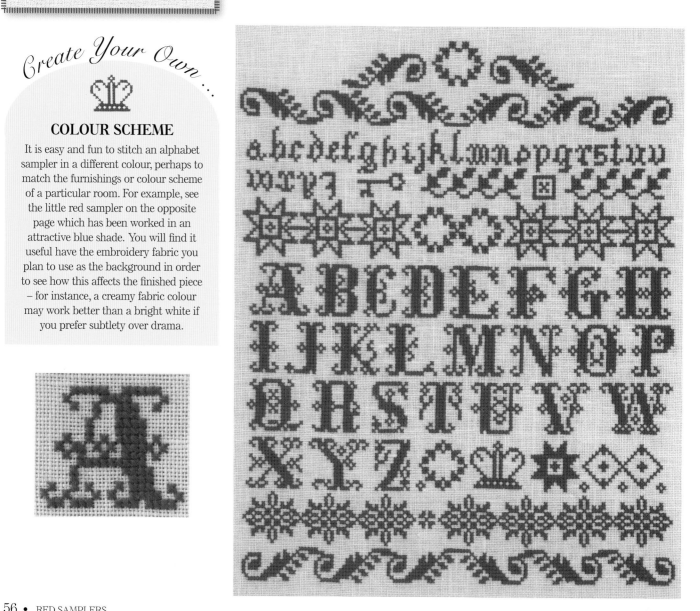

Italic Alphabet Cushion

This design is very simple to stitch on either linen or Aida fabric. It has been given extra impact by being made up as a cushion with a striking cotton lace trim but see page 100 if you prefer it as a picture.

Stitch count 90 x 169
Design size 17.5 x 33cm (7 x 13in)
You will need 30.5 x 46cm (12 x 18in) unbleached 26-count Dublin linen (Zweigart shade 11) • checked fabric and lace trim if making up as a cushion

Fold the fabric in four and mark the folds with tacking (basting) stitches. Using a loop start (page 11), work the cross stitch from the chart on page 60, starting at the centre of the chart and fabric. Work over two linen threads (or one Aida block) using two strands of stranded cotton (floss). When complete, make up as a cushion as described on page 101.

Little Red Alphabet Picture

This simple little alphabet is worked on unbleached linen and has an attractive drawn thread border, which means it needs to be worked on linen. I have also worked another version using a blue thread on ivory linen. If you prefer to work on Aida, try one of the Zweigart Vintage Aida fabrics for an antique feel. You will need to omit the zigzag hemstitch border but the design will still look charming.

Stitch count 53 x 81 excluding hemstitch border
Design size 10 x 16cm (4 x 6¼in)
You will need 30 x 36cm (12 x 14in) unbleached 26-count Dublin linen (Zweigart shade 11)

Fold the fabric in four and mark the folds with tacking (basting) stitches. Using a loop start (page 11), work the cross stitch from the chart on page 61 starting at the centre of the chart and fabric. Work over two linen threads using two strands of stranded cotton (floss). When complete, add the optional zigzag hemstitch border.

Working a zigzag hemstitch border: From the middle of one of the long sides, count four fabric threads from the edge of the stitching and using sharp, pointed scissors, cut six horizontal fabric threads. Carefully unpick the threads, working in pairs, to the edge, matching at the corners. Remove one fabric thread completely, creating a ladder in the fabric. Using a size 22 needle, re-weave the neighbouring thread into the edge of this ladder. Do not attempt to remove more than one thread at a time as the reweaving will be much less effective. Repeat on all corners. Work zigzag hemstitch (page 97) around the edge using two strands of stranded cotton (floss) that match the fabric colour. When the design is complete, stretch and mount it as a picture (see page 100).

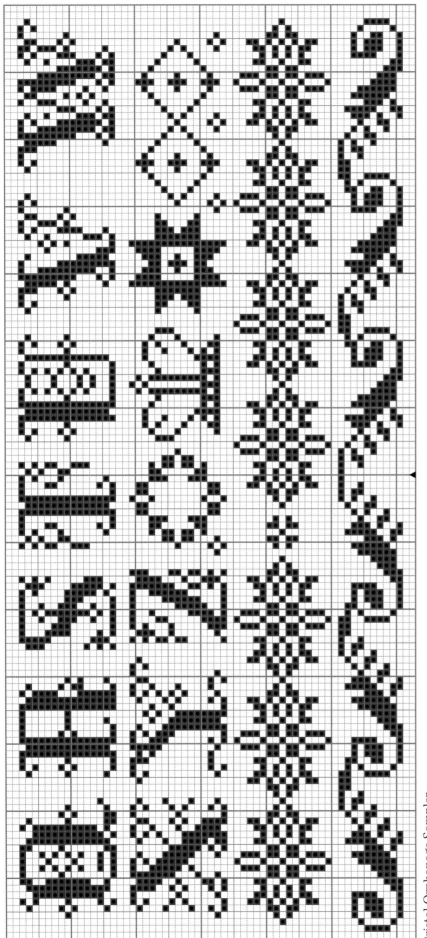

Bristol Orphanage Sampler

DMC (ANCHOR)
Cross stitch

■ 321 (9046)

Italic Alphabet Cushion

DMC (ANCHOR)
Cross stitch
■ 347 (9046)

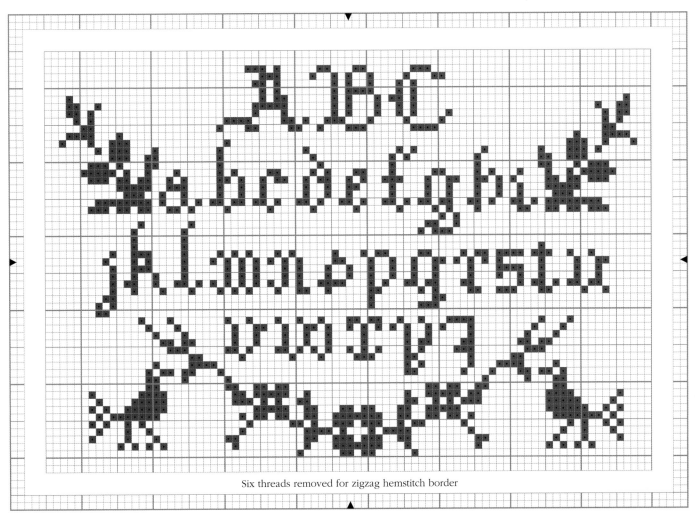

Six threads removed for zigzag hemstitch border

Little Red Alphabet Picture

DMC (ANCHOR)
Cross stitch
▣ 304 (47)

Links to the Past

George Müller was born in 1805 in Prussia (now Germany). By his own admission he was a liar and a thief who stole from his family and friends and spent time in prison. However, in November 1825 he was converted to the Christian faith and his life took a completely new track. In 1829 Müller travelled to England to work as a missionary and it was in England that he started his extraordinary work amongst the orphaned children of Bristol. In 1836, Müller opened his first house for 30 girls and over the next 35 years, he opened five orphanages on Ashley Down, Bristol, housing more than 2,000 children altogether. All Müller children were smartly dressed, well fed and educated. Boys stayed in the orphanages until they were 14, girls until they were 17. When they left the orphanage all children were found employment and given clothing and a bible.

Berlin Woolwork Samplers

I have a number of samplers worked in Berlin wool, all on canvas with unstitched backgrounds. The brightly coloured woolwork sampler by Anne Jones (above) was purchased on eBay, the auction website. Beautiful hand-painted woolwork charts first came into Britain in about 1810, with a range of Berlin woollen threads, known as such because they were produced in Berlin, an important centre for dyeing in the early 19th century. These charts are now very collectable and sought after by dealers and embroiderers.

Ann Jones' sampler is stitched on double canvas and although it is quite naïve and not particularly well stitched, it demonstrates the qualities of Berlin wools very clearly. Although stitched in 1875, it is still vivid and colourful. The unlikely flowers, animals, birds and brightly coloured baskets of fruit are delightful and I wanted to capture the lively, colourful quality of this work in my own design.

Berlin Swallows Sampler

I wanted to create a design that had the freshness, simplicity and bright colouring of Anne Jones' work, and having collected original Berlin patterns for some years it seemed an excellent idea to use some of these to compose the colourful swallows sampler shown opposite. I worked the sampler using stranded cottons (floss) rather than wools (yarns) as this is my personal preference, but you could use tapestry wools if you prefer. You will notice that the project is completely free of backstitch outline except on the swallows' breasts, as a lack of backstitch is a feature of the original Berlin patterns. The design could be stitched on evenweave or Aida fabric.

Berlin Swallows Sampler

◇◇◇◇◇◇◇◇◇◇◇◇◇◇◇◇

Stitch count 177 x 247
Design size 32 x 45cm (12½ x 17½in)

1 Fold the fabric in four and mark the folds with tacking (basting) stitches. Using a loop start (page 11), work from the chart on pages 66–69, starting at the centre of the chart and fabric.

2 Work over two fabric threads (or one Aida block) using two strands of stranded cotton (floss) for the cross stitches. Remember to keep the top stitch facing the same direction. Add the backstitch to the birds' breasts in one strand of DMC 824 (Anchor 134).

3 When the stitching is complete, check for missed stitches, remove tacking (basting) and mount and frame as preferred (see page 100). Wadding (batting) was used to give the picture an attractive padded look.

Create Your Own …

BERLIN PATTERNS

I think the secret of Berlin patterns is the choice of striking colours and the complete lack of backstitch. When planning your own stylized piece, remember to use lots of shading in leaves and petals and no backstitch! You will need a stranded cotton (floss) shade card so that you can shade successfully – these are available at craft stores or from thread manufacturers. For instance, when shading a leaf you would use four or five complementary greens to create a realistic effect.

Quartet of Berlin Flowers

I have selected four posies from the main chart to produce these exquisite little pictures. They are stitched in the same way, so there is one set of instructions, with individual stitch counts and design sizes. The designs can be worked on linen or Aida fabric and can face in any direction, so would be perfect for table linen. I worked each flower on different fabric but have used the same frame to link the group together. You could work the flowers on one piece of fabric.

Violet
Stitch count 31 x 29
Design size 5.5cm (2¼in) square
You will need candy pink 28-count Cashel linen (Zweigart shade 443)

Rose
Stitch count 30 x 30
Design size 5.5cm (2¼in) square
You will need oatmeal 28-count Perlleinen (Zweigart shade 53)

Poppy
Stitch count 30 x 29
Design size 5.5cm (2¼in) square
You will need mushroom 28-count Cashel linen (Zweigart shade 345)

Petunia
Stitch count 29 x 30
Design size 5.5cm (2¼in) square
You will need beige 14-count Zweigart linen Aida

Fold the fabric in four and mark the folds by pressing firmly. Using a loop start (page 11), work the cross stitch posy motif from the main chart on pages 66–69 starting at the centre of the charted motif and in the middle of the piece of fabric.

Once all the stitching is complete, frame as desired (see page 100). Wadding (batting) was used behind the embroideries before framing to give the pictures a nice padded look.

Links to the Past

The creation of embroidery charts in Berlin from
1835 was big business – thousands were produced. The early charts
are the best, created by skilled artists who understood canvaswork embroidery.
The designs were etched on copper plates and printed on quality paper, often beige or
grey blue. The charts were then hand coloured. When the trade was at its height, thousands
of girls were employed to do the skilful hand colouring. Originally watercolours or slightly
thicker gouache-type paints were used, and the paint was applied using a special brush
with a square end, the width of the squares on the paper.
The wool used for Berlin embroidery came from Saxony Merino sheep, which was soft and
ideal for embroidery. Change came after the invention of aniline dyes by Sir William Perkins
in England in 1856. These produced much brighter colours than had previously been
possible with natural dyes, so England soon overtook Berlin in the production of
wools. With invention of double canvas in about 1860 and the development
of the new dyes, Berlin woolwork was in its heyday.

DMC	(ANCHOR)	Cross stitch
221	(1006)	
223	(10)	
225	(271)	
327	(94)	
367	(245)	
368	(213)	
434	(351)	
436	(363)	
437	(891)	
470	(256)	
471	(279)	
550	(102)	
552	(88)	
676	(301)	
677	(386)	
712	(2)	
738	(880)	
793	(136)	
824	(134)	
931	(978)	
932	(129)	
937	(269)	
939	(152)	
3347	(239)	
3721	(29)	
3752	(1037)	
blanc	(1)	

824 (134)

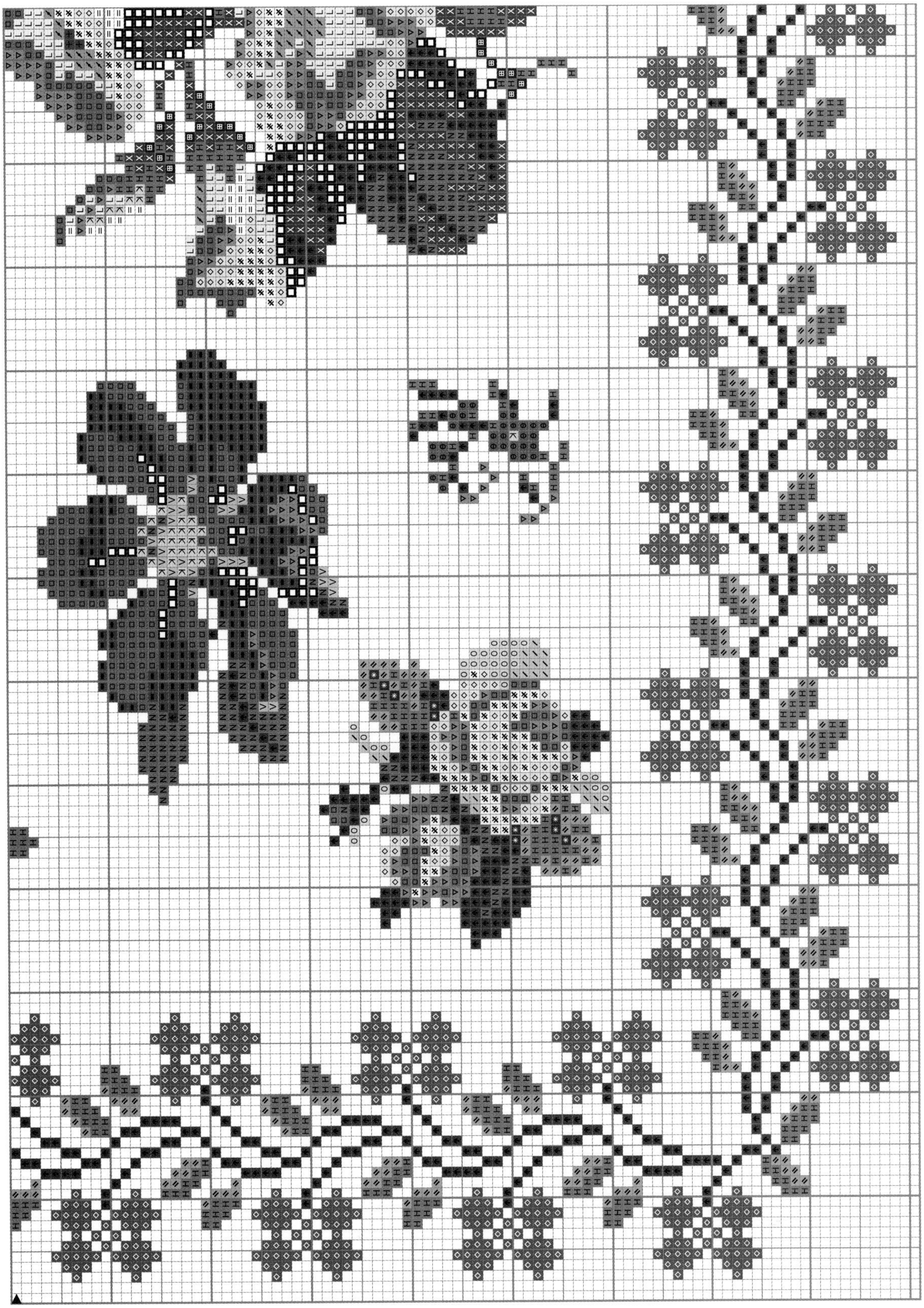

BOTTOM LEFT

DMC (ANCHOR) Cross stitch	
221	(1006)
223	(10)
225	(271)
327	(94)
367	(245)
368	(213)
434	(351)
436	(363)
437	(891)
470	(256)
471	(279)
550	(102)
552	(88)
676	(301)
677	(386)
712	(2)
738	(880)
793	(136)
824	(134)
931	(978)
932	(129)
937	(269)
939	(152)
3347	(239)
3721	(29)
3752	(1037)
blanc	(1)

824
(134)

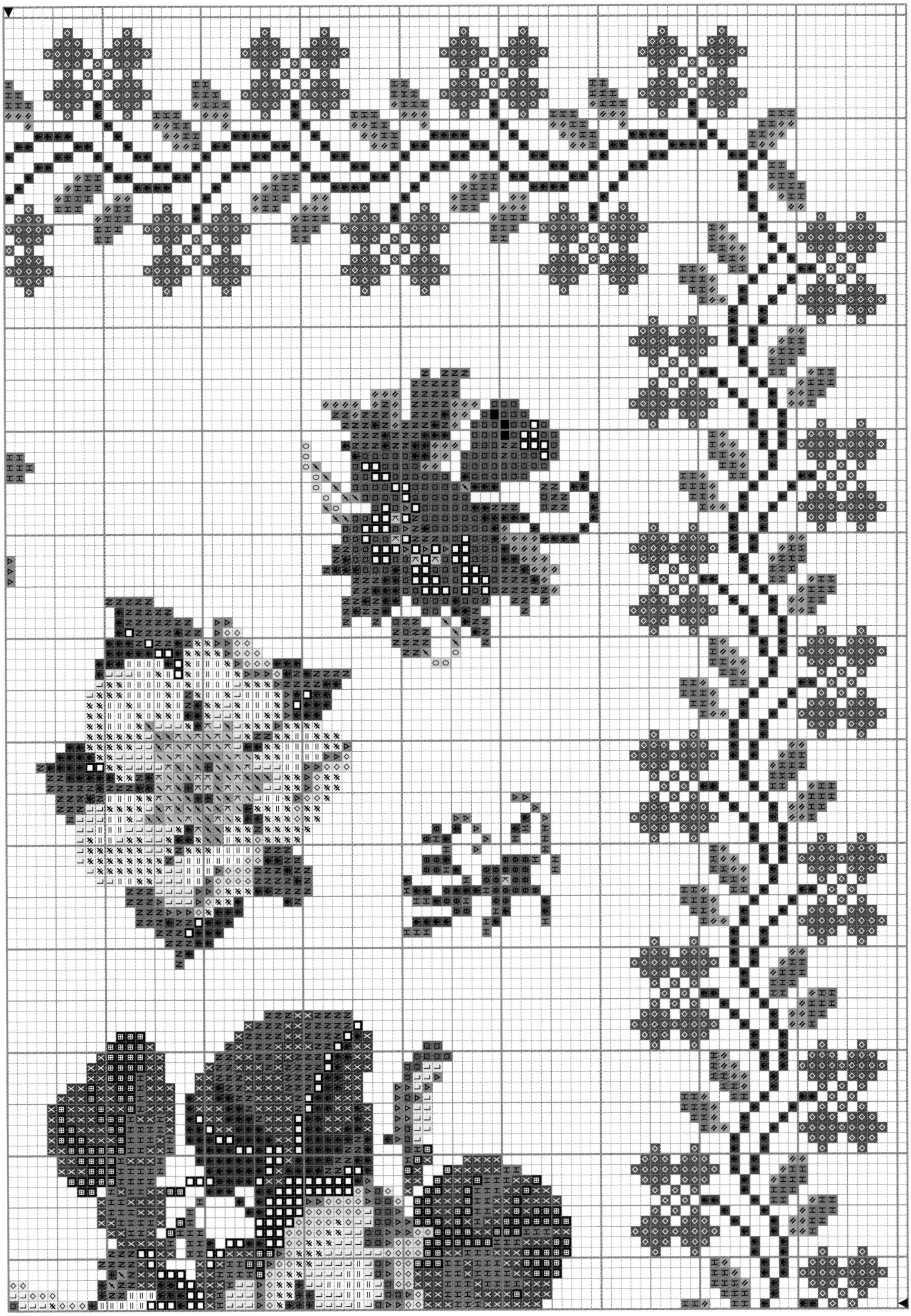

BOTTOM RIGHT

Victorian Sentiments

Upstanding Victorians loved quoting spirit-enhancing Bible texts, snippets from the *Common Prayer Book* and from the works of William Shakespeare. Children would be admonished using the Ten Commandments and Psalms, and phrases such as, 'Children should be seen and not heard'.

I have two examples of this type of stitching. One, shown above, illustrates the poem 'Home Sweet Home', the words of which (see below) were used as the lyrics of a song, first performed in 1822 in the opera *Clari, the Maid of Milan*. The other sentiment, 'Absent but not forgotten' (see page 8), includes a photograph of two rather dour-looking Victorians. My Victorian pieces are worked on stitching paper (perforated paper), formerly called Bristol Board, and are stitched in stranded cottons (floss). My own interpretation of such samplers, shown opposite, would make a cheerful and inspirational addition to any stitcher's home.

Mid pleasures and palaces though we may roam,
Be it ever so humble, there's no place like home.
John Howard Payne (1792–1852)

Wise Words Samplers

The saying 'Home Sweet Home' has become a bit of a cliché and it is certainly included in cross stitch kits more often than any other, but I still love it. My design has the addition of lovely roses, created with French knots and bullion knots. The second design was inspired by the old proverb 'A stitch in time saves nine'. We stitchers know this to be true but tend not to sew unless it is our embroidery stitching – buttons are not replaced, hems are not repaired but cross stitch continues! Both designs are straightforward to stitch and can be worked on 28-count linen as shown here, or on 14-count Aida. Refer to the Stitch Library starting on page 88 for working the stitches.

Home Sweet Home

◇◇◇◇◇◇◇◇◇◇◇◇◇◇◇

Stitch count 57 x 222
Design size 10.5 x 40cm (4 x 16in)

Neat Backstitching

Try to resist the temptation to leap across more than two threads when backstitching: the finished effect will not look as good as trailing threads will show through on the front.

1 Fold the fabric in four and mark the folds with tacking (basting) stitches. Oversew or hem the raw edges of the fabric to prevent fraying. Beginning at the centre of the chart and fabric and using a loop start (page 11), follow the chart on pages 74–75. Refer to the Stitch Library (starting on page 88) for working the stitches.

2 Work the cross stitch over two fabric threads (or one Aida block) using two strands of stranded cotton (floss), keeping the top stitch facing in the same direction. Use one strand for the backstitch following the shades given on the chart. Use two strands for the French knots in the centres of the large flowers.

3 Use a gold-plated needle to create the rose motifs on the capital letters, working two or three French knots in pale yellow DMC 677 (Anchor 386) in the positions marked on the chart, with curly bullion knots around them in pink and dark pink (see detail above). After the roses have been formed, add the leaves in counted chain stitch by eye in two strands of green DMC 470 (Anchor 256).

4 When stitching is complete, check for missed stitches, remove tacking (basting) and mount and frame as preferred (see page 100), using wadding (batting) to create a nice padded look.

Floral Spray Coaster

You can work this simple but decorative coaster using the corner motif from the main chart on page 74. The pretty pulled-thread edging is created with four-sided stitch. If you stitch a set of four coasters they can be arranged on the table facing in any direction.

Stitch count 45 x 67
Design size 8.2 x 12cm (3¼ x 4¾in) excluding pulled-thread border
You will need
20 x 23cm (8 x 9in) ivory 28-count Zweigart linen

Fold the fabric in four and mark the folds with lines of tacking (basting) stitches. Start with a loop start (page 11) and stitching over two fabric threads, work the motif in the corner of the fabric, approximately 2.5cm (1in) from the fabric edges, using two strands of stranded cotton (floss) for cross stitch and one for backstitch.

To edge the coaster, count four threads from the outermost stitch on each side and work a border of four-sided stitch over two threads (see page 91) using two strands of DMC ecru (Anchor 387) stranded cotton (floss). Count fourteen threads from the outside of the four-sided stitch and withdraw the fifteenth fabric thread. Cut along the withdrawn thread with sharp shears and then press firmly on the wrong side with a hot iron and using spray starch to slightly stiffen the coaster. To finish, fray the raw edge all round to within four threads of the square-stitched edge. Remove the tacking (basting).

A Stitch in Time

◇◇◇◇◇◇◇◇◇◇◇◇◇◇◇

Stitch count 54 x 202
Design size 10 x 37cm (4 x 14½in)

1 Fold the fabric in four and mark the folds with tacking (basting) stitches. Beginning at the centre of the chart and fabric and using a loop start (page 11), follow the chart on pages 76–77. Refer to the Stitch Library for working the stitches.

2 Work the full and three-quarter cross stitch first over two fabric threads (or one Aida block) using two strands of stranded cotton (floss) and keeping the top stitches facing in the same direction. Use one strand for the backstitch using the shades given on the chart.

3 To add the little skein of thread by the thimble motif, use a dressmaker's pin and pick up five fabric threads. Using two strands of thread on your needle, wind orange DMC 740 (Anchor 925) around the pin in a figure-of-eight movement several times and before moving the pin, anchor the bundle in position with contrasting thread.

4 When the stitching is complete, check for missed stitches, remove tacking (basting) and mount and frame (see page 100) using wadding (batting).

Create Your Own ...

VICTORIAN TEXT

If you have a favourite saying, text or perhaps a family motto, you could recreate a Victorian feel by working the design on parchment-coloured stitching paper. You could even chart some of the amusing stitchers' laments if you prefer something more modern. If using charting software, you can type in your words, select a font and it will chart it for you. As you can see from the photograph on page 70, the antique text is worked on stitching paper in cross stitch and long stitch. When working on paper, avoid using fractional stitches.

Stork Case

This pretty case will hold a pair of spectacles or pens and pencils with ease. It has been adapted from the main design but has its own chart on page 99. The design is only suitable for working on linen if you want to work the attractive folded hem.

Stitch count 31 x 90   **Design size** 5.6 x 16.5cm (2¼ x 6½in) front flap only
You will need 25 x 25cm (10 x 10in) 28-count Zweigart Perlleinen (shade 53)

Fold the fabric in three equal parts and mark the folds with tacking (basting) stitches. Start stitching from the centre of the chart and the centre of the top part of the fabric (this will be the front of the case). Use a loop start (page 11) and working over two fabric threads, work cross stitch using two strands of stranded cotton (floss) and backstitch with one strand. When all the stitching is complete, check for missed stitches, remove tacking (basting) and press firmly on the wrong side using spray starch to slightly stiffen the fabric.

To create the folded hem, refer to page 93 for detailed instructions. To make up the stork case, fold the bottom flap up and slipstitch the side edges to the middle part of the fabric with matching thread.

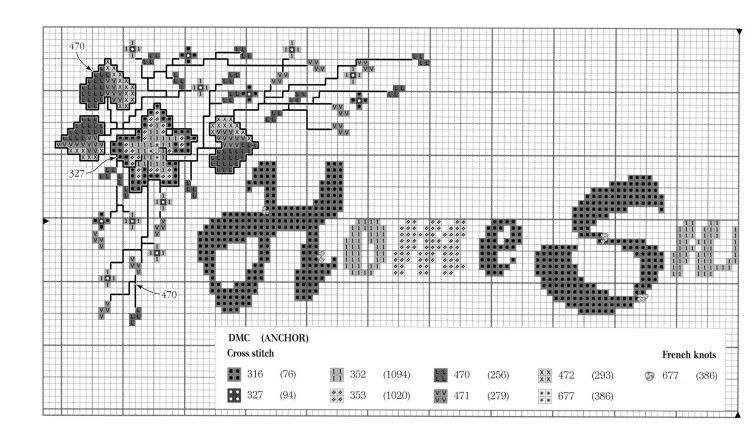

DMC   (ANCHOR)

Cross stitch   **French knots**

■ 316	(76)	⊞ 352	(1094)	▨ 470	(256)	⊠ 472	(293)	◉ 677	(386)
⊡ 327	(94)	◩ 353	(1020)	⊻ 471	(279)	✳ 677	(386)		

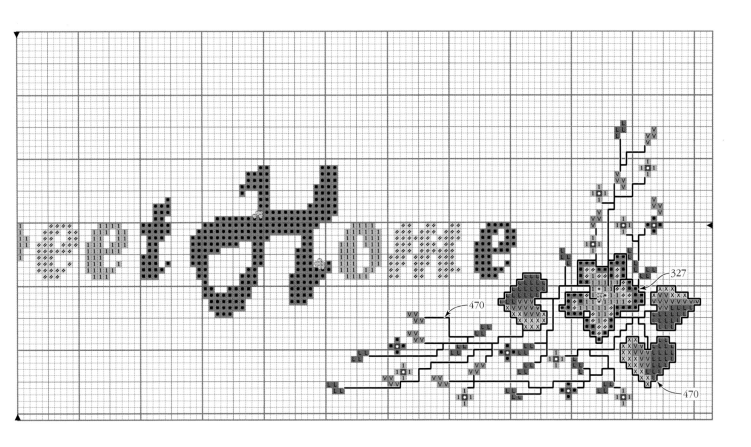

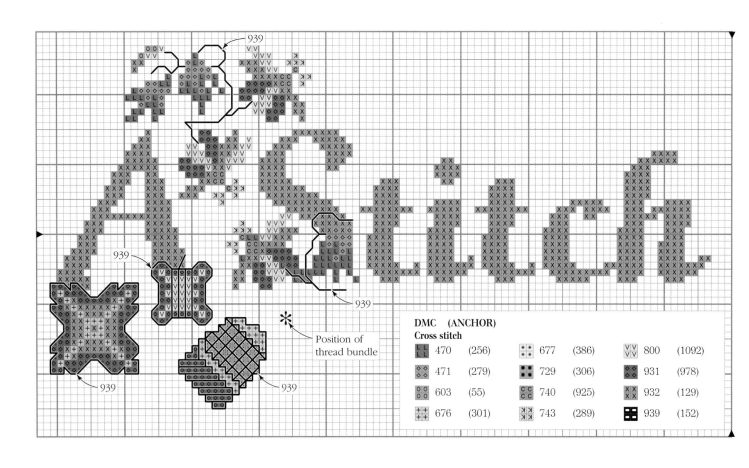

DMC (ANCHOR)
Cross stitch

LL	470	(256)	677	(386)	VV 800 (1092)
471	(279)	729	(306)	931 (978)
603	(55)	CC 740	(925)	XX 932 (129)
++ 676	(301)	743	(289)	939 (152)

939

Position of
thread bundle

Band Samplers

This section looks at one of my favourite sampler groups, band samplers, one of the most fascinating areas of early embroidery. The antique band sampler (above) has been kindly lent by a friend and is simply exquisite. Worked in 1649 on linen, it is extremely valuable and I wish it were mine! I love the little 'boxer' figures with the wonderful top knots and the dogs at their feet.

Band samplers, long strips of linen, were not intended to be decorative but to be a stitcher's aide-mémoire. Patterns were copied and stitches practised and when not in use, the strip was rolled up and put in a draw for safekeeping. The 'bands' could include dozens of different stitches. Antique band samplers are very collectable and can cost a fortune at auction and so are out of reach of most stitching enthusiasts. This is an opportunity to work your own antique-style sampler for a fraction of the cost!

Band Sampler Collection

Inspired by the many bands and stitches on the antique sampler, I have chosen to work four small band samplers rather than a large one but you could combine the motifs and bands on to one fabric piece. One sampler focuses on blackwork patterns and motifs and uses some gold metallic thread, while the delicately coloured strawberries and cream sampler has various bands of drawn and pulled thread work giving it a lovely lacy feel. The other two samplers are collections of my favourite motifs and bands and include some additional counted stitches to add texture and an antique feel. Two of the samplers have folded hem borders worked before framing and all four need to be worked on evenweave fabric. Refer to the Stitch Library for working all the stitches used.

Blackwork Band Sampler

Stitch count 150 x 36
Design size 27 x 6.5cm (10¾ x 2½in)

For this band sampler I have used the traditional blackwork combination of black and gold but do experiment with other colours. Many different effects can be achieved by varying the thickness of the threads used and careful selection of patterns with dark, medium and light tones. Refer to the Stitch Library (pages 88–97) for working all the stitches used.

1 Fold the fabric in four and mark the folds with tacking (basting) stitches. Using a loop start (page 11), work the row of herringbone stitches just below the centre. Work a line of tacking (basting) stitches, under and over two linen threads at either end of this completed band: these will indicate the edges of the sampler and should be removed when all work is finished.

2 Using one strand of stranded cotton (floss), work all the blackwork patterns in Holbein stitch or double running stitch in black or metallic gold, according to the chart. Use the gold metallic thread in short lengths to avoid excessive wear on the thread.

3 Using two strands of thread, work the eyelets, Algerian eyes, double cross stitch, Rhodes stitch, French knots, bullion knots and herringbone stitch.

4 When the stitching is complete, check for missed stitches, remove tacking (basting) and mount and frame as preferred. Wadding (batting) was used to give the sampler an attractive padded look. If you wish to create a hemstitched edge, as shown on the Carnation and Butterfly sampler on page 82, follow the instructions on page 93.

Links to the Past

Blackwork is an embroidery technique of geometric patterns built up using Holbein stitch (also called double running stitch) and was traditionally worked in black thread against a contrasting (usually white) background with gold metallic highlights added for extra impact. During Elizabethan times, it was used to decorate clothing to imitate the appearance of lace although the name is a little misleading as this type of counted embroidery can be stitched in any colour. Holbein stitch (named after the painter) produces a smooth effect, so the back of your work will look almost as good as the front, making it useful for table linen.

Strawberries and Cream Band Sampler

◇◇◇◇◇◇◇◇◇◇◇◇◇◇◇◇◇◇

Stitch count 150 x 35
Design size 29 x 6.8cm (11½ x 2¾in)

You will need

40 x 20cm (16 x 8in) pale unbleached 26-count Dublin linen (Zweigart shade 52)

Stranded cotton (floss) as listed in the chart key

Madeira gold metallic thread No.15 shade 22

Tapestry needle size 26

This delicate pulled and drawn thread sampler is simpler to stitch than it seems if you take it in short stages. The chart and instructions are divided into banded areas to help you work through.

1 Fold the fabric in four and mark folds with tacking (basting) stitches. Work the top band at least 5cm (2in) from the top of the fabric to allow for making up.

2 Using a loop start (page 11), begin working the bands over two linen threads, unless stated otherwise.

Band 1: work the cross stitch, tipsy stitch and half Rhodes stitch using two strands of stranded cotton (floss). Work a line of tacking (basting) stitches, under and over two linen threads at either end of this completed band: these indicate the edges of the sampler and will be removed later.

Band 2: work the hemstitch square following the instructions on page 48. I added my initials in dove's eye stitches but you could work any pattern you like. Work the lines of couched gold above and below the hemstitched square.

Band 3: work zigzag hemstitch, ladder hemstitch then zigzag again, as follows. Working from the centre of the band, snip the horizontal linen threads down the centre line once and, using a needle,

un-pick the threads back to the band edge (see chart for how many threads are removed). Working in pairs, remove one thread completely and reweave the other into the gap (see diagram, bottom page 92), continuing until all threads are removed or re-woven. Following the chart, hemstitch the remaining fabric threads using two strands of stranded cotton (floss).

Band 4: work the slightly smaller hemstitch square in the same way as band 2, adding dove's eyes in the pattern shown (or one of your choice). Work the four-sided stitch over two threads.

Band 5: work the bands of hemstitch (ladder, zigzag then ladder again) as in band 3, then the diamond hemstitch. Add rows of counted chain stitch and herringbone stitch using two strands of thread in the colours given.

Band 6: work the strawberry using two strands for cross stitch and one for back-stitch. Use two strands for the queen stitch and four-sided stitch over four threads.

Band 7: cross stitch the heart outlines in two strands, then add the pulled satin stitch in the centres (one vertically and the other horizontally), working across two threads, one thread apart and pulling the stitches very firmly. Work a row of hemstitch after four threads removed. Work the cross stitch motifs using two strands, backstitch with one and detached buttonhole stitch, bullion knots and French knots with two strands. Work vertical herringbone patterns in two strands in the colours given.

3 When stitching is complete, remove tacking (basting) and mount and frame, using wadding (batting) for a padded look and silk moiré behind the embroidery to emphasize the pulled thread work. To create a hemstitched edge, as in the Carnation and Butterfly sampler overleaf, see page 93.

Carnation and Butterfly Band Sampler

Stitch count 143 x 38
Design size 23 x 6cm (9 x 2½in)

This colourful and fine sampler is very satisfying to work and includes a butterfly worked over one thread of the linen where you may need your magnifier! Refer to the Stitch Library (pages 88–97) for working all the stitches used.

1 Fold the fabric in four and mark the folds with tacking (basting) stitches. The top band needs to be worked at least 5cm (2in) from the top of the fabric to allow for making up.

2 Using a loop start (page 11), begin working the bands over two linen threads, unless stated otherwise.

Band 1: work the cross stitch and French knots using two strands of stranded cotton (floss), adding the backstitch in one strand in the colours given on the chart.

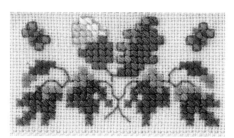

Band 2: work the hemstitch by removing four threads and working the top row. Work the backstitch motifs with one strand and then the butterfly (charted separately) in one strand and over only *one* thread. Work the bullion rose and the French knots in the centre with two strands. Work the needlelace leaves with the French knots in the centre in two strands. Repeat the hemstitching and withdrawn threads to finish this band.

Band 3: work the cross stitch with two strands and backstitch with one. Work the zigzags of tipsy stitch with two strands, followed by the vertical threaded backstitch using two strands for the backstitch and one for the weaving.

Band 4: work the hemstitch as in band 2. Go on to work the cross stitch with two strands and backstitch with one. Work the satin stitch squares using two strands, following the stitching directions on the chart. Complete each section of satin stitch before moving on. Work the queen stitches with two strands, followed by threaded backstitch, using one strand for the backstitch and two for the weaving.

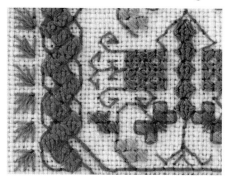

3 When stitching is complete, check for missed stitches, remove tacking (basting) and mount and frame. Alternatively, create a hemstitched edge following the instructions on page 93.

Violets and Berries Band Sampler

Stitch count 147 x 38
Design size 26.5 x 7cm (10½ x 2¾in)

You will need

40 x 20cm (16 x 8in) cream
28-count Vintage Cashel linen
(Zweigart shade 1019)

Stranded cotton (floss)
as listed in the chart key

Madeira gold metallic thread
No.15 shade 22

Tapestry needle size 26

I have used a special Zweigart fabric for this pretty little sampler to give it an antique feel. Knowing that many stitchers enjoy creating antique-style samplers, Zweigart have invented a technique to give the fabric an aged appearance. There are a number of these Vintage fabrics available both in evenweave and Aida.

1 Fold the fabric in four and mark folds with tacking (basting) stitches. Work the top band at least 5cm (2in) from the top of the fabric to allow for making up.

2 Using a loop start (page 11), begin working the bands over two linen threads, unless stated otherwise.

Band 1: work the Vandyke stitch over four threads using two strands of stranded cotton (floss). Use two strands for the half eyelets, then work the backstitch patterns with one strand.

Band 2: work the cross stitch, queen stitch and French knots with two strands and the backstitch with one. Work the diamond hemstitch, removing four threads, leaving four threads and removing four. Work the ladder hemstitch with four threads removed.

Band 3: work cross stitch and backstitch as before, then the threaded backstitch with one strand for the backstitch and two strands for the weaving. Work Montenegrin stitch with two strands.

Band 4: work cross stitch, queen stitch and backstitch as before. Work Pekinese stitch with two strands of each colour.

Band 5: work the gold metallic couching, then cross stitch and backstitch as before. Work the hemstitched rectangles, removing the threads indicated on the

chart and working the hemstitch as shown (see diagrams page 87). Decorate remaining threads with needleweaving – I worked a triangular pattern in each half of the hemstitched square but you could work a different pattern.

Band 6: work the cross stitch, queen stitch and tipsy stitch using two strands, adding backstitches in one strand.

Band 7: work the four-sided stitch and quarter eyelets in two strands and the Vandyke stitches over six threads using two strands. Work the diamond hemstitch as in band 2 but leave the upper row as ladder hemstitch.

3 When stitching is complete, remove tacking (basting) and mount and frame, using wadding (batting) for a padded look and silk moiré behind the embroidery to emphasize the pulled thread work. To create a hemstitched edge, as shown, see page 93.

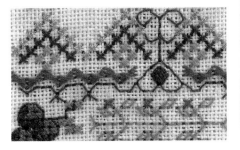

eyelet in black

Holbein stitch blackwork patterns
in black and gold

Algerian eye with French knot
in black

Holbein stitch in gold thread

gold thread couched in black

double cross stitch in black

gold thread couched in black

French knots in black

backstitch in black

Rhodes stitch in black

backstitch in black

bullion knots in black

French knots in black

gold thread couched in black

herringbone stitch in black

gold thread couched in black

gold thread couched in black

double cross stitch in black

gold thread couched in black

Rhodes stitch in black

Holbein stitch in gold thread

gold thread couched in black

gold thread couched in black

Blackwork Band Sampler

DMC	(ANCHOR)
Cross stitch	
▦ 310	(403)
▩ Madeira metallic gold	

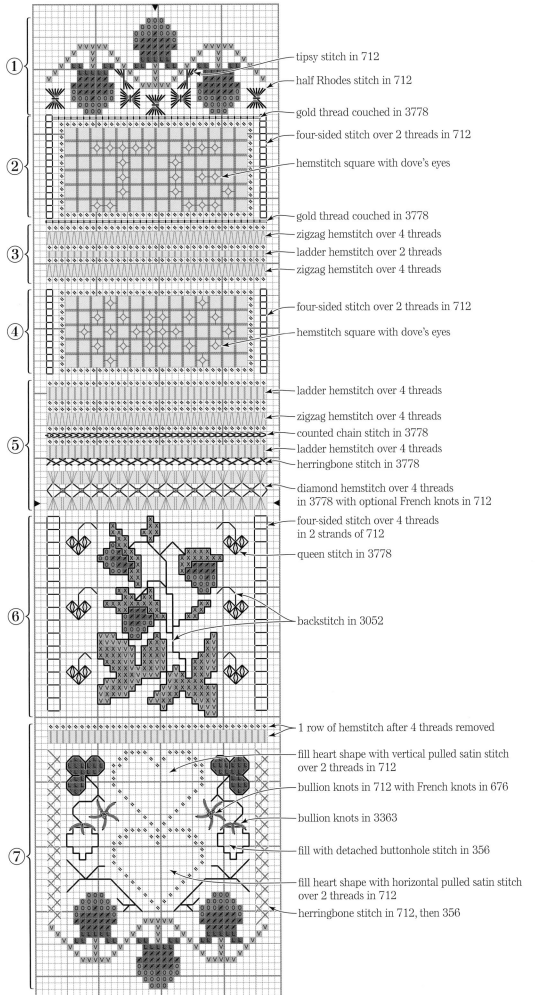

① tipsy stitch in 712

half Rhodes stitch in 712

gold thread couched in 3778

② four-sided stitch over 2 threads in 712

hemstitch square with dove's eyes

gold thread couched in 3778

③ zigzag hemstitch over 4 threads

ladder hemstitch over 2 threads

zigzag hemstitch over 4 threads

④ four-sided stitch over 2 threads in 712

hemstitch square with dove's eyes

ladder hemstitch over 4 threads

zigzag hemstitch over 4 threads

counted chain stitch in 3778

ladder hemstitch over 4 threads

herringbone stitch in 3778

⑤ diamond hemstitch over 4 threads
in 3778 with optional French knots in 712

four-sided stitch over 4 threads
in 2 strands of 712

queen stitch in 3778

backstitch in 3052

⑥

1 row of hemstitch after 4 threads removed

fill heart shape with vertical pulled satin stitch
over 2 threads in 712

bullion knots in 712 with French knots in 676

bullion knots in 3363

fill with detached buttonhole stitch in 356

fill heart shape with horizontal pulled satin stitch
over 2 threads in 712

⑦ herringbone stitch in 712, then 356

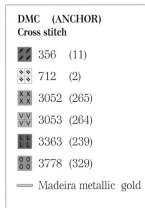

DMC (ANCHOR)
Cross stitch

	356	(11)
	712	(2)
	3052	(265)
	3053	(264)
	3363	(239)
	3778	(329)

— Madeira metallic gold

🌀 French knots in
colours as labelled

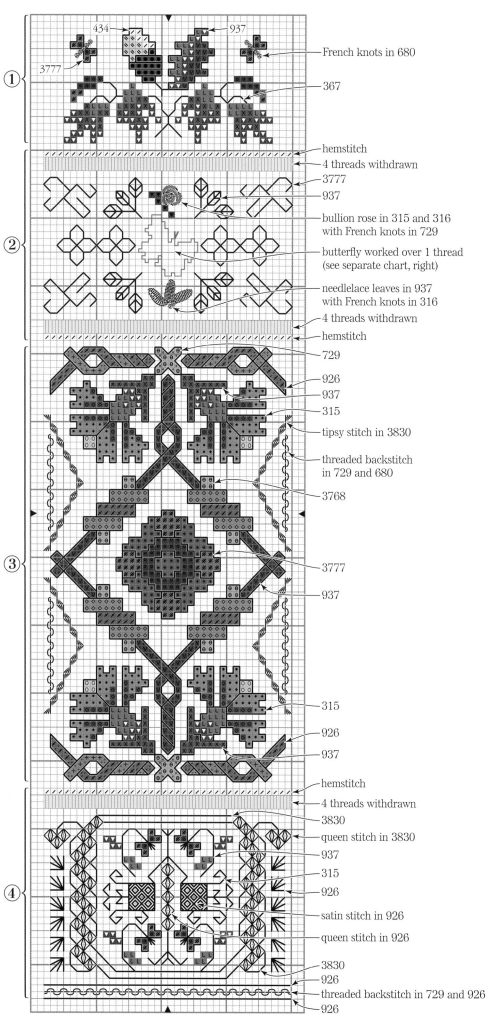

① 434   937

3777

French knots in 680

367

hemstitch

4 threads withdrawn

3777

937

bullion rose in 315 and 316
with French knots in 729

butterfly worked over 1 thread
(see separate chart, right)

needlelace leaves in 937
with French knots in 316

4 threads withdrawn

hemstitch

729

926

937

315

tipsy stitch in 3830

threaded backstitch
in 729 and 680

3768

3777

937

315

926

937

hemstitch

4 threads withdrawn

3830

queen stitch in 3830

937

315

926

satin stitch in 926

queen stitch in 926

3830

926

threaded backstitch in 729 and 926

926

Carnation and Butterfly
Band Sampler

DMC (ANCHOR)
Cross Stitch

315 (65)   926 (208)

316 (76)   937 (269)

356 (11)   3051 (268)

434 (351)   3346 (245)

470 (256)   3768 (877)

680 (307)   3777 (20)

712 (2)   3830 (29)

729 (306)

738 (880)   ✿ French knots
as labelled

778 (103)

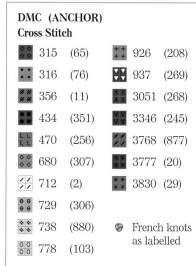

Butterfly motif (cross stitched over
1 thread, i.e., 1 square equals 1 thread)

434
(351)

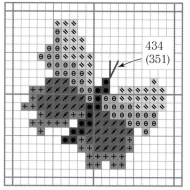

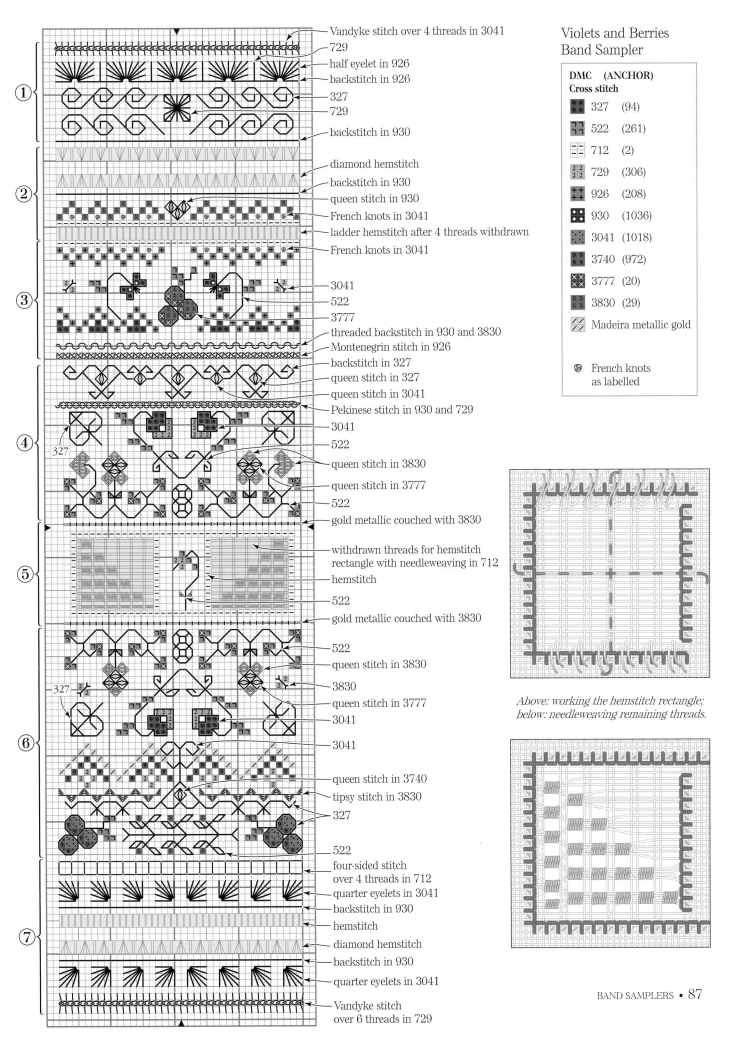

Vandyke stitch over 4 threads in 3041
729
half eyelet in 926
backstitch in 926
327
729
backstitch in 930

diamond hemstitch
backstitch in 930
queen stitch in 930
French knots in 3041
ladder hemstitch after 4 threads withdrawn
French knots in 3041

3041
522
3777
threaded backstitch in 930 and 3830
Montenegrin stitch in 926
backstitch in 327
queen stitch in 327
queen stitch in 3041
Pekinese stitch in 930 and 729
3041
522
queen stitch in 3830
queen stitch in 3777
522
gold metallic couched with 3830

withdrawn threads for hemstitch
rectangle with needleweaving in 712
hemstitch
522
gold metallic couched with 3830

522
queen stitch in 3830
3830
queen stitch in 3777
3041
3041

queen stitch in 3740
tipsy stitch in 3830
327

522

four-sided stitch
over 4 threads in 712
quarter eyelets in 3041
backstitch in 930
hemstitch
diamond hemstitch
backstitch in 930
quarter eyelets in 3041
Vandyke stitch
over 6 threads in 729

327
327

Violets and Berries Band Sampler

DMC (ANCHOR)
Cross stitch

	DMC	(ANCHOR)
	327	(94)
	522	(261)
	712	(2)
	729	(306)
	926	(208)
	930	(1036)
	3041	(1018)
	3740	(972)
	3777	(20)
	3830	(29)
	Madeira metallic gold	

French knots
as labelled

*Above: working the hemstitch rectangle;
below: needleweaving remaining threads.*

Stitch Library

◇◇◇◇◇◇◇◇◇◇◇◇◇◇◇◇◇◇◇◇◇◇◇◇◇◇◇◇◇◇◇◇◇◇

The stitches used in this book are described here alphabetically. In many cases the stitches may be worked on Aida, evenweave or canvas unless stated otherwise, although I would not recommend working pulled stitches on Aida. I find it useful to have a scrap of 20-count fabric at hand to practise new stitches on before working them on a project. Some of the diagrams show the stitch worked over two or four fabric threads. Many diagrams give a numbered stitching sequence. Remember, when working a stitch, the construction stays the same but the size and number of fabric threads used may alter, so refer to the project and chart for the correct number of threads involved. When constructing a stitch, remember which way you worked and keep all the stitches the same, clockwise or anticlockwise.

Algerian Eye

This pretty star-shaped stitch is a pulled stitch, which means that when it is formed correctly holes are pulled in the fabric. It can be worked over two or four threads of evenweave and is more successful worked on evenweave than Aida.

1 Start to the left of a vertical thread and work from left to right around each stitch in an anticlockwise direction (or vice versa but keeping each stitch the same).

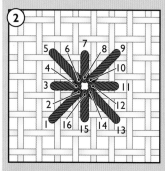

2 Always work the stitch by passing the needle down through the central hole, pulling quite firmly so that a small hole is formed in the centre. Take care that trailing threads do not cover this hole as you progress to the next stitch.

Backstitch

Backstitch is used for outlining a design or part of a design, to add detail or emphasis, or for lettering. It is usually indicated on a chart by solid lines with the shade code indicated on the chart or key. Backstitch is added after the cross stitch has been completed, to prevent the backstitch line being broken by the cross stitches. See page 97 for working threaded backstitch.

To work backstitch, follow the number sequence in the diagram, working over one block of Aida or two threads of evenweave, unless stated otherwise on the chart. Avoid long, loose stitches unless for flower stamens and so on.

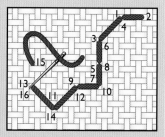

Bullion Stitch – bars and roses

This is a very versatile stitch that can be formed in straight bars or in curves to form roses, as seen in Home Sweet Home on page 72. I don't attempt these stitches unless using a gold-plated needle.

Straight Bullion Bar

1 The stitch is begun by working an incomplete backstitch, leaving the needle in the fabric. It is vital that the point of the needle exits from the hole where it started.

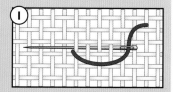

2 With the needle still in the fabric, wind the thread around the needle as many times as necessary to make the coil the length of the incomplete backstitch. Hold the needle and coil of thread firmly against the fabric, then gently pull the needle through the coil and fabric. Using a gold-plated needle makes this exercise much smoother. To finish the bullion bar turn the coil back on itself and push the needle through the fabric at the rear of the backstitch.

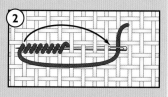

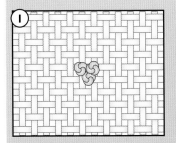

Bullion Rose

1 First work a couple of French knots as described on page 91. Now work a bullion bar, adding extra winds to the needle to force the bar to bend.

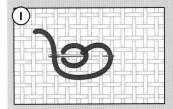

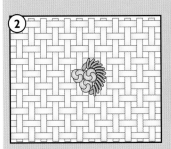

2 Begin to build up the rose, adding more tightly curved bullions around the first curved bar.

3 The completed bullion rose above has six curved bullions, with the colour changed to a deeper shade on the final two but you can change their shape and colour as desired.

Buttonhole Stitch

This very old stitch is simple to work and extremely versatile. It is used as the basis for detached buttonhole stitch (below right).

Start with an away waste knot (page 11) and follow the numbered sequence in the diagram here. Buttonhole stitches are usually worked closely together but may be spaced more widely according to the pattern you are working.

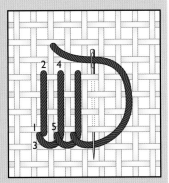

Button Loop

To create a button loop, useful for fastening the needle fold on page 24, work four straight stitches in and out of the same hole and then bring the needle to the surface at one end. Working on top of the fabric and just under the straight stitches, work buttonhole stitches all along the bar, closely together.

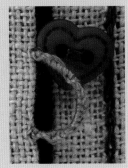

Couching

This is not a counted stitch as such but can be very effective, particularly on a band sampler (see page 80). It is often worked with a metallic thread laid on the fabric, held down by small vertical stitches. Start by bringing the laid thread up through the fabric and laying it across the fabric. Using the couching thread, work small vertical stitches, as shown.

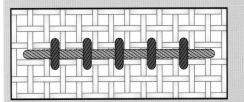

Counted Chain Stitch

This stitch is very versatile as it may be used on evenweave or Aida, as part of a pattern, as an outline, in close rows to fill a pattern or to join sections of stitching together.

1 To work chain stitch on evenweave, start to the left of a vertical thread, bringing the needle up through the fabric and down through the same hole, forming a loop on the surface. Pass the point of the needle under two threads and up to the surface forming another loop. Each new stitch thus anchors the previous stitch.

2 If chain stitch is worked as a border, then the last stitch will anchor the first. If not, the last stitch may be anchored over one thread, as shown here.

Cross Stitch

Refer to page 12 of Back to Basics for working cross stitch and three-quarter cross stitch on Aida and evenweave.

Detached Buttonhole Stitch

This stitch can be used to fill shapes, such as the strawberries in the band sampler on page 81. The stitches should lie closely together but are shown more widely spaced on the right side of the second diagram overleaf to explain the stitch more easily. The rows are worked to and fro, with the first and last stitches of each row worked into the fabric, to anchor all the buttonhole stitches.

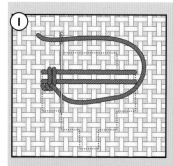

1 Begin by outlining the motif in backstitch, then work two long stitches across the width of the shape. Work the first row of buttonhole over this satin stitch line.

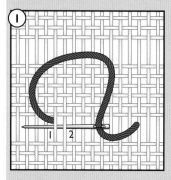

2 When you come to the end of the row, reverse direction and work the next row into the previous row, with the stitches close together. Continue working to and fro, reducing the length of the rows to follow the shape being filled.

Diamond Hemstitch

This is an attractive hemstitch variation (see hemstitch, page 92). Withdraw threads either side of a solid fabric area (see withdrawing and reweaving threads, page 92) and then work the hemstitch in two journeys. The stitches will form diamond shapes on the front of the work and if pulled firmly will create small holes in the solid fabric area. The trick to remember with this stitch is that it is formed on the front of the fabric, so if you find yourself with the needle on the back you know something is wrong!

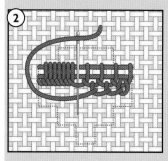

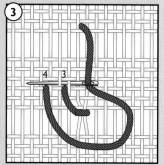

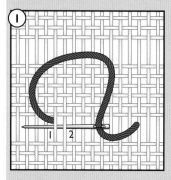

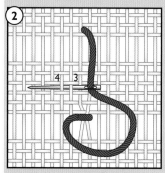

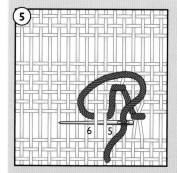

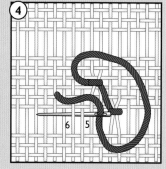

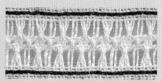

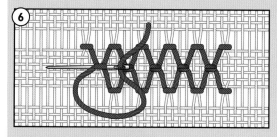

Double Cross Stitch

Double cross stitch can be worked over two or four threads of an evenweave fabric or over one or two blocks of Aida, to create a series of bold crosses or stars. Tiny double cross stitches may be formed over two threads of evenweave but they are difficult to work on one block of Aida. To keep all double cross stitches uniform make sure that the direction of the stitches within them is the same.

To work, start to the left of a vertical thread and following the numbered sequence in the diagram, work a diagonal cross stitch and then add a vertical cross on top. The second vertical cross may be worked in a different colour to add interest, in which case work the stitch in two stages – all lower crosses first, followed by the top crosses.

Dove's Eye Stitch

This is a traditional Hardanger stitch usually constructed whilst needleweaving or wrapping. It is used in the band sampler on page 81. The diagrams here show Kloster blocks worked but these aren't required for this book.

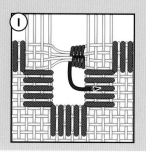

1 Whilst working the last side of a square, needleweave to the centre of the bar, bringing the needle out through a void area, as shown.

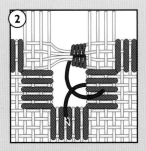

2 Pierce the neighbouring needlewoven bar or wrapped thread halfway along its length, bringing the needle up through the void and through the loop formed by the thread.

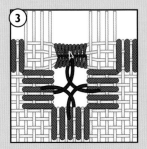

3 Continue round the square following the diagram sequence but before resuming needleweaving, loop the needle under the first stitch to form the final twist in the dove's eye.

Eyelets

These can be stitched in various shapes, as shown here and the rules are the same for all eyelets: as with Algerian eye you need to pass the needle down the central hole, working the stitch in the correct sequence (numbered on the diagrams) and in one direction to ensure that the hole is round and uniform. Take care that trailing threads do not cover the hole as you progress to the next stitch.

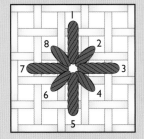

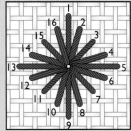

Four-Sided Stitch

This is traditionally worked as a pulled stitch to create a lacy effect without the removal of fabric threads. It can also be used as a hemstitch when threads are to be cut or removed. The secret of creating a perfect four-sided stitch is to make sure that your needle travels in the correct direction on the back of the stitch. The stitches on the front should be vertical or horizontal but diagonal on the back. It is this tension that forms the small holes as the stitch is worked. The stitch is not recommended for Aida fabric.

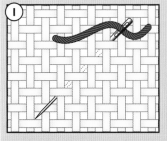

1 Begin to the left of a vertical thread and work a horizontal straight stitch across four threads (or number on the chart), passing the needle diagonally across four threads at the back of the work.

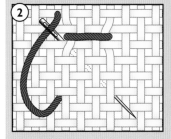

2 Bring the needle up and form a vertical straight stitch, again passing the needle diagonally across four threads at the back of the work.

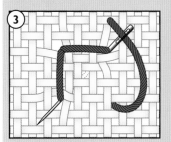

3 Bring the needle up and form another vertical straight stitch, again passing the needle diagonally across four threads at the back.

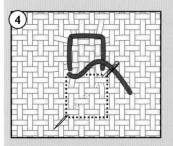

4 Work a horizontal straight stitch to form the last side of the square but this time pass the needle across diagonally to begin the next stitch.

French Knot

French knots are small but important stitches though they can cause distress as they are apt to disappear to the back of the work or end up as a row of tiny knots on the thread in the needle! Follow the steps below for perfect knots.

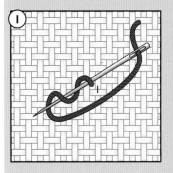

1 Bring the needle through to the front of the fabric and wind the thread around the needle twice. Begin to 'post' the needle partly through to the back, one thread or part of a block away from the entry point (to stop the stitch being pulled to the wrong side).

2 Gently pull the thread you have wound so that it sits snugly at the point where the needle enters the fabric. Pull the needle through to the back and you should have a perfect knot in position. If you want bigger knots, add more thread to the needle as this gives a better result than winding more times round the needle.

Half Eyelet

This is worked in a similar way to a full eyelet (page 91) but only completing one half.

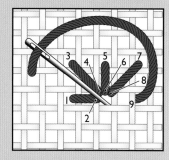

Half Rhodes Stitch with Bar

This is an adaptation of Rhodes stitch (page 96), producing a decorative stitch shaped rather like a sheaf of corn, with a straight bar across the centre to tie the threads together. Buttonhole stitching could be added to the bar.

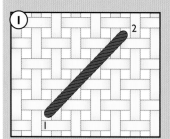

1 Work over squares of two, four, six or eight threads of evenweave fabric (or according to the chart) in a slanting, anticlockwise direction.

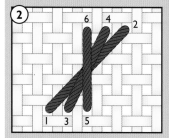

2 Complete the half Rhodes stitch by following the numbered sequence on the diagrams, and maintain the same sequence for every stitch to achieve a uniform effect.

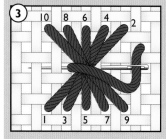

3 To finish the Rhodes stitch, add a single straight stitch across the centre, holding all the threads firmly.

Hemstitch

Hemstitch is wonderfully versatile, allowing you to hem raw edges, form folded hems (see right) or remove horizontal threads and decorate the verticals in various ways. When working hemstitches for the first time it is simple to work them without removing threads first, eliminating the anxiety of cutting too many, although traditionally the threads are removed before the hemstitching. When you have perfected the stitch you can experiment with thread removal – see withdrawing and reweaving threads, below.

A hemstitch is made up of parts – two straight stitches and one diagonal on the back. It is this combination that forms the safe barrier if threads are to be cut or removed. If you are intending to cut to the edge, you may prefer to use double hemstitch where each stage of the stitch is worked twice. Hemstitch can look very effective worked in rows without any threads removed. The stitch is not suitable for Aida.

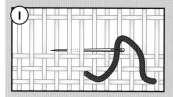

1 This shows hemstitching over two threads in each direction. Begin by working a straight stitch across two threads, turning the needle to face horizontally.

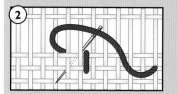

2 Make a straight stitch across two threads, at right angles to the first stitch, then pass the needle down diagonally under two threads.

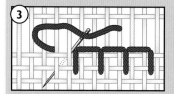

3 Repeat the straight stitches along the row, counting carefully.

Withdrawing and Reweaving Threads

To remove horizontal threads prior to hemstitching, count carefully to the centre of the band and cut horizontal threads down the centre line (refer to the chart for how many threads to cut). Using a needle, un-pick the linen threads back to the edge of the band. Working in pairs, remove one thread completely and then reweave the other into the gap (see ladder hemstitch, page 93). Continue until all the threads are removed or rewoven. Following the instructions on the chart, hemstitch the remaining fabric threads using two strands of stranded cotton (floss).

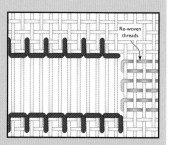

Re-woven threads

Stitching a Folded Hem

Many projects are beautifully finished off by a folded and stitched hem – such as the band samplers on page 82 and 83. This method is also used for the needle fold on page 24 and could be used for table linen.

1 From the middle of the long side (of a sampler) count five threads out from the edge of the stitching and cut the sixth thread. Carefully unravel this thread back to the corner and reweave it into the margin. Repeat on all four sides. Now lay the fabric wrong side up on a hard surface and count out from the missing thread to the ninth and tenth threads. Place the point of a tapestry needle between these threads and pull the fabric (not the needle) to score a line that will form a crease – this will form the fold at the edge of the work. Repeat on all four sides.

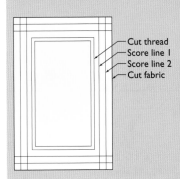

Cut thread
Score line 1
Score line 2
Cut fabric

2 Score the fabric again, nine threads further out (line 2 on the diagram, left). Score another line seven threads out and cut the fabric carefully following this line of threads.

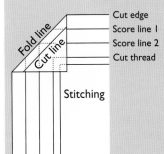

Cut edge
Score line 1
Score line 2
Cut thread
Fold line
Cut line
Stitching

3 Fold the fabric piece at the corners and cut as shown in the diagram, left Now fold in all the edges, mitring the corners.

4 Hemstitch the folded edge in place as shown in the diagram below. At the corners, stitch the mitres with invisible stitching up the seam.

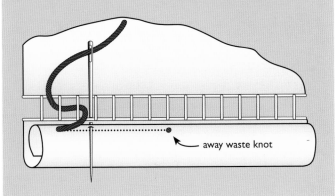

away waste knot

Herringbone Stitch

This simple and decorative stitch is often used on band samplers, making a fine companion to cross stitch. It looks particularly pretty when combined with stitches like long-legged cross stitch. It can also be whipped with a second colour. It is shown here worked over four evenweave threads diagonally and under two horizontally. It can be worked over two and under one to make it smaller, or over and under more threads to make it larger.

Work the stitch by starting to the left of a vertical thread, across the number of threads indicated on the chart, following the numbered sequence in the diagram.

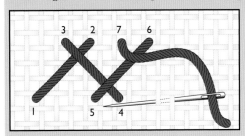

Holbein Stitch

This stitch, also called double running stitch, is the stitch used for blackwork, which looks the same on the back and front. Backstitch creates a rather padded and untidy reverse. Holbein stitch can be worked in two colours by changing colour before completing the gaps on the return journey.

Work a row of running stitch in one direction, counting to ensure that you work under and over two threads of evenweave or one Aida block, and then back over the row in the opposite direction, filling in the gaps.

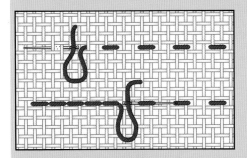

Ladder Hemstitch

This is the simplest decorative hemstitch. Cut the horizontal threads (see withdrawing and reweaving threads, page 92) and reweave them, as shown. Work two rows of hemstitch as described on page 92 – the vertical threads that remain form a ladder pattern.

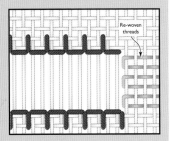

Re-woven threads

Long-Legged Cross Stitch

This stitch, also known as long-armed Slav stitch and Portuguese stitch, looks wonderful when worked in rows because it forms a plaited effect ideal for borders, or for the outside edges of pieces to be made up as a pincushion or a scissor keeper. It can also be worked on Aida across two blocks and upwards over one. The stitch can also be used to join sections.

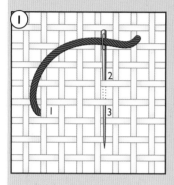

1 To work long-legged cross stitch on evenweave, begin to the left of a vertical thread. Following the numbered sequence, insert the needle four threads forwards and two threads upwards in a long diagonal 'leg'.

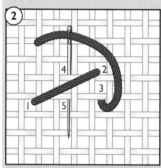

2 Insert the needle two threads upwards and two threads backwards diagonally to make the short leg.

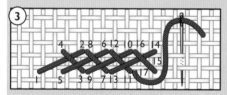

3 To work a row of long-legged cross stitch, follow the sequence in this diagram.

Montenegrin Stitch

This unusual stitch looks similar to long-legged cross stitch but is constructed differently and includes an extra vertical leg, which gives it a fuller appearance. It forms an embossed braid on the front of the stitching and makes a raised edge for folding. It is shown worked on evenweave but can also be worked on Aida by moving two blocks forward and one up.

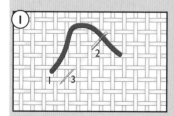

1 Start to the left of an evenweave thread, and following the numbered sequence in the diagram, work a long diagonal leg by moving four threads forwards and two threads up. Bring the needle two threads back and two threads down to emerge at 3.

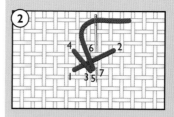

2 Insert the needle two threads backwards diagonally to make the short leg at 4. Bring the needle back up at 5 and down at 6 to form the final vertical leg.

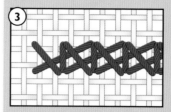

3 Repeat Montenegrin stitch in a row to form the pattern shown.

Needlelace

I have used needlelace to create leaves on the band sampler on page 82 but needlelace is not a modern idea – some 17th-century samplers included pretty flower petals created this way. The technique isn't difficult but practising on spare fabric helps. The instructions that follow show petals being worked but the principle is the same for leaves.

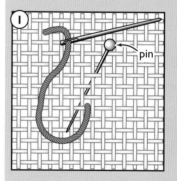

1 Begin by positioning a glass-headed pin in the material as shown in Fig 1. If using stranded cotton (floss), anchor a pair of threads using the loop start method. If using one strand of perlé cotton, use an away waste knot.

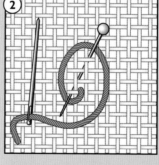

2 Wind the thread around the pin as shown here.

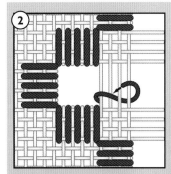

2 Beginning from a cut area, bring the needle up through a void area.

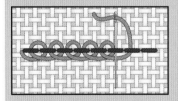

3 Weave the needle under and over pairs of threads to form a plaited effect. The stitches should not distort or bend the threads.

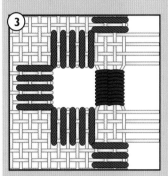

3 Wind the thread around the pin again and stop winding when you are at the head of the pin.

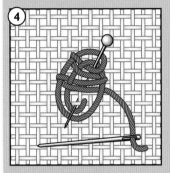

4 Using the needle, weave in and out of the threads. It takes a little practice to get an even finish but it is very effective. When a petal or leaf is complete, pass the needle to the wrong side and remove the pin. Repeat the process to make as many petals or leaves as you need.

5 When the flower or leaf spray is complete, add some French knots to the centre, or as indicated on the chart.

Pekinese Stitch

This looped stitch is worked over a line of backstitch and may use two different types of thread and two colours. To explain the stitch more clearly, the loops are shown loosely worked in the diagram below but can be pulled tighter to achieve different effects.

Work a line of backstitch the width of the area to be stitched. Take the interlaced thread from left to right, passing it beneath the second backstitch, then looping to pass beneath the third and so on, but not piercing the fabric.

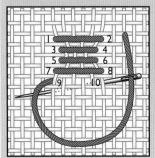

Needleweaving

Needleweaving is used to decorate the loose threads that remain either when threads are cut as in Hardanger embroidery or when fabric areas have had threads removed. The needleweaving creates covered bars and these can be decorated with stitches like picots, while the spaces between bars can be filled with decorative stitches such as dove's eyes and spider's webs. The diagrams show Kloster blocks worked but these aren't required for this book – see the band sampler on page 87 (band 5).

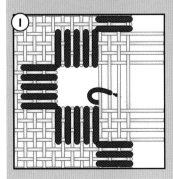

1 Start by anchoring the thread under adjacent cross stitch or hemstitch on the back of the work.

Pulled Satin Stitch

Pulled satin stitch is worked in the same way as normal satin stitch (page 96) but the threads are pulled as you stitch, which forms holes in the fabric and creates a lacy effect.

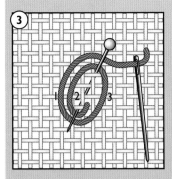

Queen Stitch

This stitch is made of four parts and forms little dimples in the embroidery by pulling small holes in the fabric. It is gorgeous when worked as a group. The stitch is traditionally worked from right to left, but if you find this difficult to count, work the two middle parts first followed by the outer ones.

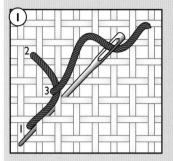

1 Work one long stitch over four threads of the fabric, which is then moved two threads to the right by the needle coming up at 3 and a small stitch worked across one thread.

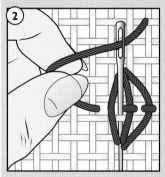

2 Repeat the long stitch from the same position as in Fig 1, but this time bending the stitch over one thread only.

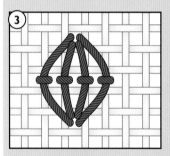

3 Repeat the long stitch from the same position as in Fig 1, but this time the long stitch is bent to the left and the needle re-enters the fabric in the centre position.

4 The last stage of the stitch is completed forming a lantern shape on the fabric. Note how the top and bottom hole is shared by each stage of the stitch so forming the holes or little dimples that make this stitch so distinctive.

Rhodes Stitch

Rhodes stitch produces a solid, slightly raised, three-dimensional effect, almost like a series of studs on the fabric. The diagrams that follow illustrate one version but the size of the stitch can be altered – check the chart to see how many threads are in each stitch. This stitch doesn't work well on Aida fabric.

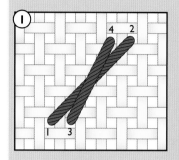

1 Begin to the left of a vertical evenweave thread, working each stitch over squares of two, four or more threads.

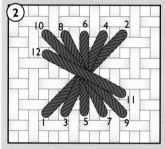

2 Following the numbered sequence, build up the stitch, working in an anticlockwise direction around the square.

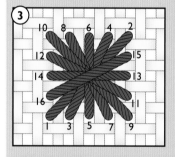

3 A correctly formed Rhodes stitch should have a raised central area. Maintain the same sequence for every stitch to produce a uniform effect.

Satin Stitch

This long, smooth stitch is often used to fill in shapes and can also look very effective when worked in blocks facing in different directions. It can be worked diagonally, horizontally or vertically.

To work satin stitch, start with an away waste knot (page 11). Beginning to the left of a vertical thread, follow the numbered sequence in the diagram, laying flat stitches side by side. Always come up the same side and down the other so the back of the fabric is covered and the stitches lie closely and neatly beside each other. Take care not to pull too tight (unless working pulled satin stitch – see page 95).

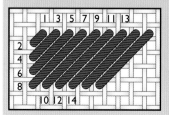
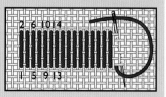

Threaded Backstitch

Sometimes called embellished backstitch, this pretty addition to backstitch is very simple to work. Work backstitch as shown on page 88 and then take the second thread colour and weave it in and out of each backstitch, creating smooth S-shaped loops. The pattern lines can be straight, as shown below, or in any pattern you choose.

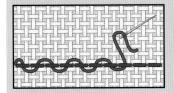 

Tipsy Stitch

This is my variation on Rhodes stitch, which is very simple to work and produces an interesting 'tipsy' slant to your stitching.

Work the stitch over two, four, six or eight threads of evenweave fabric, according to the chart. Simply follow the numbered sequence in the diagram.

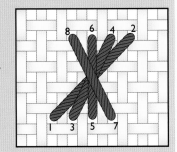

Vandyke Stitch

This stitch is quite straightforward but don't pull the stitches too tightly or you will lose the effect of the central plait. It can be worked over two, four or six fabric threads.

Bring the thread through at 1, make a small horizontal stitch at 2 and put the needle back through at 3. Now bring the thread through at 4 and without piercing the fabric, pass the needle under the crossed threads at 2 and insert at 5.

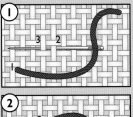
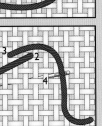
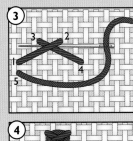

Zigzag Hemstitch

This is formed in almost the same way as ladder hemstitch (page 93). Cut the horizontal threads (see withdrawing and reweaving threads, page 92) and reweave them, as shown. Work one row of hemstitch as for ladder hemstitch and then work the second row but offset the stitches by one fabric thread to create a zigzag effect.

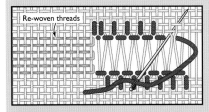 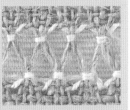

Re-woven threads

Wrapped Bars

Like needleweaving, wrapped bars may be worked alone to decorate the threads that remain after cutting or withdrawing and as part of other decorative stitches. The number of wraps depend on the project – you may only need two wraps per section as in hemstitch squares or to completely cover the bar as in Hardanger embroidery. The diagrams show Kloster blocks worked but these aren't required for this book.

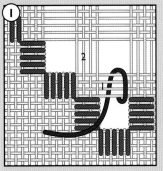

1 Start by anchoring the thread under adjacent hemstitches and then begin wrapping the fabric threads, working horizontally across the fabric. In the spot sampler on page 53, I only wrapped the threads twice.

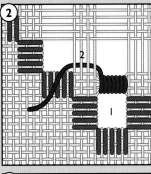

2 Wind the thread around and around the remaining fabric threads, then travel to the next group of threads and repeat. As you wrap each bar, hold the threads you are wrapping quite firmly to prevent them unravelling as you work.

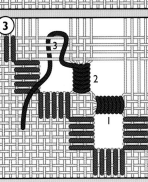

3 Continue wrapping the bars, noting how many times each set is wrapped and keeping the stitches as consistent as possible.

Additional Charts

Hedgerow Heart Sachet (page 17)

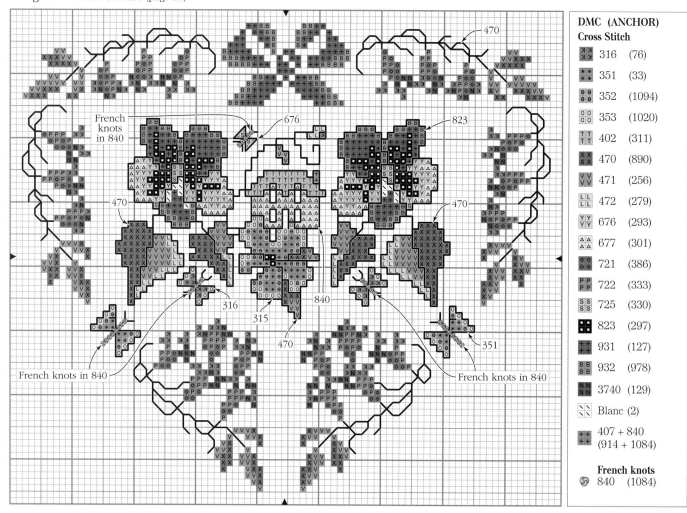

DMC (ANCHOR)		
Cross Stitch		
⊠⊠	316	(76)
✳✳	351	(33)
⊚⊚	352	(1094)
○○	353	(1020)
T T	402	(311)
✕✕	470	(890)
V V	471	(256)
L L	472	(279)
Y Y	676	(293)
△△	677	(301)
◌◌	721	(386)
P P	722	(333)
S S	725	(330)
▪▪	823	(297)
▩▩	931	(127)
B B	932	(978)
N N	3740	(129)
╲╲	Blanc	(2)
✚✚	407 + 840 (914 + 1084)	
French knots		
✺	840	(1084)

Fanciful Flowers Alphabet (page 24)

DMC (ANCHOR)	
Backstitch	
—	3011 (277)
(or colour of your choice)	
French knots	
✺	3011 (277)
(or colour of your choice)	

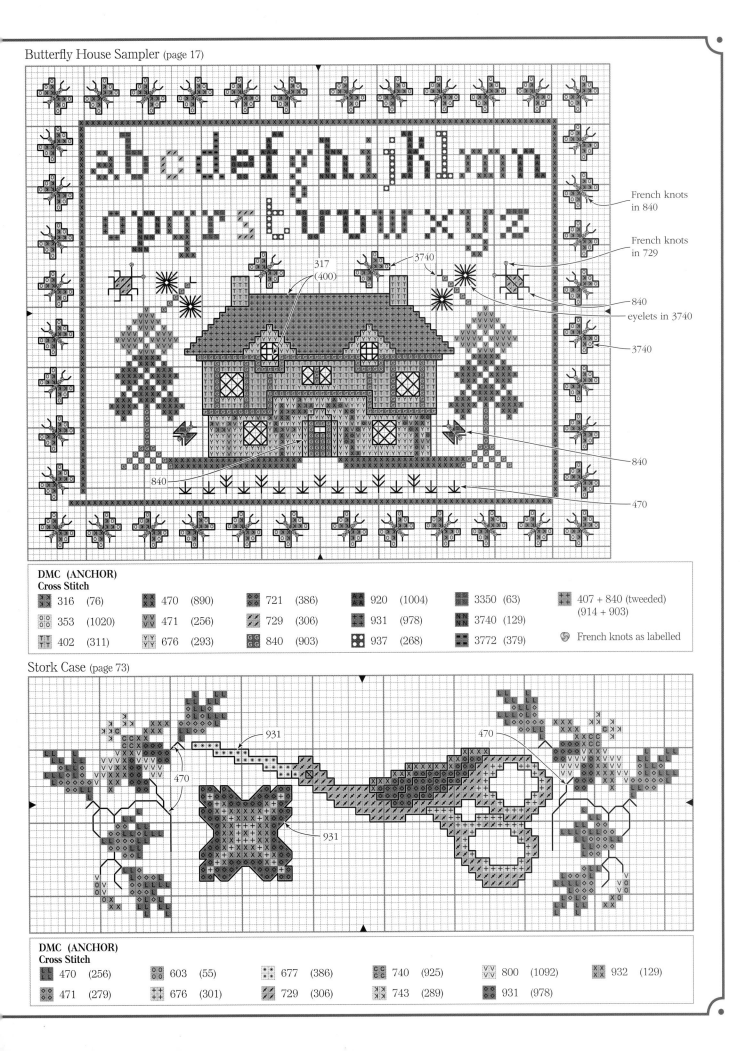

Butterfly House Sampler (page 17)

French knots in 840

French knots in 729

840

eyelets in 3740

3740

840

470

317 (400)

3740

840

DMC (ANCHOR)
Cross Stitch

316 (76)	470 (890)	721 (386)	920 (1004)	3350 (63)	407 + 840 (tweeded) (914 + 903)	
353 (1020)	471 (256)	729 (306)	931 (978)	3740 (129)		
402 (311)	676 (293)	840 (903)	937 (268)	3772 (379)	French knots as labelled	

Stork Case (page 73)

931

470

470

931

DMC (ANCHOR)
Cross Stitch

470 (256)	603 (55)	677 (386)	740 (925)	800 (1092)	932 (129)
471 (279)	676 (301)	729 (306)	743 (289)	931 (978)	

Finishing & Making Up

◇◇◇◇◇◇◇◇◇◇◇◇◇◇◇◇◇◇◇◇◇◇◇◇◇◇◇◇◇◇◇◇◇◇◇◇◇

How your embroidery is finished and made up makes a great deal of difference to the look of the piece. This section describes some of the finishing techniques used in this book.

Stretching and Mounting

Your embroidery will look its best if stretched and mounted. When mounting small cards or novelty items you can use double-sided adhesive tape, but it is worth taking more time and effort on larger projects.

All the framed embroidery in this book has been mounted using polyester wadding (batting) to create a padded finish. The advantage of this is that any slightly lumpy bits on the back of your work will be pushed into the padding rather than appear as raised areas on the front. The padding also raises the embroidery, which displays it to better effect.

The two band samplers on pages 81 and 83 have been mounted with the addition of silk moiré. A fabric stretched under the embroidery in this way creates a colour and texture contrast which displays hemstitching to better effect and also emphasizes other areas of pulled and drawn thread work.

There are three methods of attaching your embroidery to board before framing:
• Pin the work to a fabric-covered board and then stitch it into position.
• Pin the work to the edge of the board and stick in place with double-sided adhesive tape.
• Pin the work to the board and lace across the back both ways with strong linen thread.

To stretch and mount an embroidery on a fabric-covered board you will need either acid-free mounting board or lightweight foam board or foamcore.

1 Using a sharp craft knife, cut a piece of foamcore board to fit your frame – an easy way to do this is to cut round the glass that fits the frame.

2 Trim the wadding (batting) to the same size as the foamcore and attach it to the foamcore using double-sided tape. Position your embroidery on top of the wadding and centre it carefully in relation to the board. Fix the embroidery in position by pinning through the fabric into the board edges. Start in the middle of each side and pin towards the corners, making sure your pins follow a line of Aida holes or a linen thread so that edges will be really straight. If necessary, adjust the fabric's position until it is centred and straight.

3 Turn the work over and, leaving pins in place, trim excess fabric to 5cm (2in) all round.

Framing

You will see from some of the wonderful photographs in this book, that the way in which a design is framed can greatly affect the end appearance. Mounting and framing by a professional can be expensive, particularly if you want something a little different, but most of the finishing techniques suggested in this book can be tackled at home.

When choosing a frame for a particular project, select the best moulding you can afford. Generally embroidery looks better framed without glass but if you prefer glass use crystal glass, which although more expensive will minimize reflections and distortions. You must also ensure that the embroidery does not get squashed by the underside of the glass. Either use a spacer (narrow strips of board), gold slip, or a mount (mat) between the glass and the mounted embroidery to hold them apart. Adding a single mount or double mount can add dimension to even the simplest project. Framers have a large selection of mounts in all sizes and colours or will cut one to fit. Ask the framer to make up the frame and a coloured or gold slip for you, but buy the frame, glass and so on in kit form (most framers do not mind!) and then put it together yourself.

To frame your stitching, stretch and mount as described above and set aside. Place the frame face down on a covered surface and after cleaning both sides of the glass, place the glass in the frame rebate and insert the gold slip, mount or spacer followed by the stitching. Before fixing in the backboard and sealing the frame, line the inside with aluminium foil, which will discourage thunder flies from finding their way in!

Making Bias Binding

The Stitcher's Nécessaire on page 25 is completed using bias binding, which can be purchased or homemade. To make bias binding, cut strips of fabric 4cm (1½in) wide across the grain of the fabric and machine sew them together to make the length needed.

To attach bias binding by hand or machine, first cut the binding to the correct length. Pin the binding to the wrong side of the project, matching raw edges and machine or hand stitch. Now fold the binding to the right side and top stitch in position. Press lightly.

Making an Inset Cushion

An inset front to a cushion gives it a professional touch and really sets off the embroidery as you can see in the Italic Alphabet Cushion. I have used some antique checked linen and matching lace to great effect.

1 Measure the embroidery and decide on the size of the finished cushion. Allowing 1.25cm (½in) seam allowances, cut the embroidery to the required size plus two seam allowances. Press the embroidery face down on soft towels.

2 Measure the short side of the trimmed embroidery and cut two strips of fabric to match. Find the mid-point of each edge by folding and marking with a pin. Fold the border pieces in half to find the centre point and mark with a pin. With right sides together, pin the border panels to the embroidery, matching the centre points. Machine stitch these seams and press seams open.

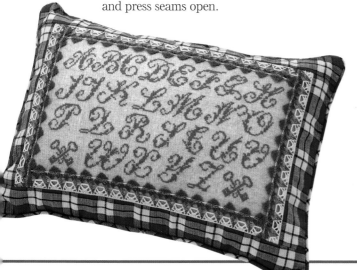

3 Measure the long side of the embroidery and cut two strips of fabric to match. With right sides together, pin the border panels to the embroidery, matching centre points. Machine stitch these seams and press open.

4 Cut backing fabric to fit your cushion front. Place the front and back right sides together and sew a seam round all edges, leaving a gap for turning. Turn through to the right side, insert a cushion pad and slipstitch the gap. In the version illustrated I added the lace trim by hand after the border pieces were completed.

Making Cards

There are many card blanks available from needlecraft shops and mail-order companies or you can make your own using pretty papers, card and ribbon, as I have for the Flower Heart card and the Traveller's Tales card on page 33.

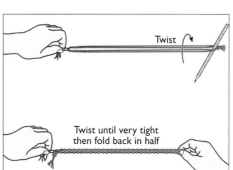

In all cases, cut the finished embroidery to the required size (allowing for fraying the edges if appropriate) and then select a coloured card that complements your threads. Create a single-fold card and embellish it with decorative paper. Attach the embroidery to the card with double-sided adhesive tape and add trims or other embellishments as desired.

Making a Twisted Cord

A twisted cord is perfect for embellishing projects – see the bookmark on page 41. Choose a colour or group of colours in stranded cottons (floss) to match your embroidery. Cut a minimum of four lengths at least four times the finished length required and fold in half. Ask a friend to hold the two ends while you slip a pencil through the loop at the other end. Twist the pencil and continue twisting until kinks appear. Walk towards your partner and the cord will twist. Smooth out the kinks from the looped end and secure with a knot at the other end.

Twist

Twist until very tight
then fold back in half

Making a length of twisted cord from embroidery threads.

Caring for Antique Samplers

◇◇◇◇◇◇◇◇◇◇◇◇◇◇◇◇◇◇◇◇◇◇◇◇

I have been collecting antique embroidery for over 20 years and still love every piece in my collection. Antique embroideries, particularly samplers have become very collectable and therefore more valuable. As a result, it is even more important that we care for any that we find and that we preserve embroidery using current knowledge and expertise. With antique textiles there are a few golden rules. I have included some examples from my collection to illustrate some of these do's and don'ts.

 The large red sampler (see frontispiece picture) had been framed very badly, with the inadequate mount actually obscuring some details of the embroidery in the bottom right of the sampler.

 Sarah Hubbard's sampler (see page 46) had a number of moth holes but these were disguised by stitching the sampler on to unbleached linen and mounting it sympathetically.

 During its restoration the very early Mary Fowler sampler (see page 7) was stitched on to well-washed unbleached linen and the linen mounted over card. The frame has spacers to keep the crystal glass away from the stitching.

The Ann Tipper sampler (see page 5) had, unfortunately, been washed, which was such a shame as some of the colours ran and these are difficult if not impossible to remove.

Map samplers are becoming very collectable and therefore more expensive to buy. I was very lucky to see my first map of England in an antique shop in a parlous state for a bargain price. It needed considerable conservation and loving care and I still love it!

✔ **Do** use acid-free card when mounting embroideries.

✔ **Do** use crystal glass where possible to avoid distortion.

✔ **Do** consider having damaged embroidery mounted on to unbleached linen to minimize faults.

✔ **Do** use spacers or mounts (mats) to keep the glass from pressing on the stitching.

✔ **Do** add aluminium foil to the back before making up the frame, to discourage insects.

✘ **Don't** attempt to wash any old embroideries – the threads were originally dyed using natural dyes and may disintegrate when the fabric comes in contact with water. This is a specialist job! De-ionized water is used by experts.

✘ **Don't** expose embroideries to sunlight.

✘ **Don't** fold embroideries – the fabric may tear on the folds. Leave flat or roll instead.

✘ **Don't** allow the embroidery to remain in contact with glass when the piece is framed as the glass could permanently damage the stitching.

Further Reading

The New Anchor Embroidery Series (David & Charles, 2005)
BISHOP, E. *A Collection of Beautiful Stitches* (Cross 'N' Patch, 2002)
DILLMONT, Therese *DMC Library: The Encyclopaedia of Needlework* (Bracken, reprinted 1987)
The Embroiderer's Guild *Making Samplers* (David & Charles, 1993)
GREENOFF, Jane *The Cross Stitcher's Bible* (David & Charles, 2000)
McNEILL, Moyra *Pulled Thread Embroidery* (Dover Publications, 1999)
O'STEEN, D. *The Proper Stitch* (Symbol of Excellence Publishers Inc, 1994)
SNOOK, Barbara *Embroidery Stitches* (Batsford, 1972)

Acknowledgments

As always, there are many people involved with the production of a book like this one, but I would like to mention a few people to whom I am most grateful. Without the support of my family, particularly my husband Bill, it would be simply impossible to continue writing cross stitch books. His patience in the face of more late meals, a tired and ratty wife and too many late nights is never ending. To my parents, Eric and Pat Fowler who continue to search out my books and magazines and make sure they are on the front of the book stand wherever they are!

My heartfelt thanks to the following: to Sue Hawkins whose continues to support me in her work as Technical Director of the Cross Stitch Guild and for her friendship, which even survives working together! To my right-hand woman, Helen Beecroft, who supports and protects me when I'm scribbling and Daphne, who keeps the business going in my absence. To John and Lucy Evans for the loan of the lovely, extremely valuable band sampler on page 78.

Many thanks to my marvellous team of stitchers and pattern testers – Hanne Fentiman, Lesley Clegg, Jill Vaughan, Margaret Cornish, Margaret Pallant, Susan Bridgens, Deborah Buglass, Liz Burford, Jacqueline Davies, Doreen Ely, Elizabeth Edwards, Jean Fox, Joyce Halliday, Joan Hastewell, Janet Jarvis, Margaret Locke, Sue Smith, Suzanne Spencer, Joan Barnes, Sue Heeley, Jane King and Joan Winwood. Jemma McMinn at Artistuff for the framing.

Thanks to all the generous suppliers of the materials and equipment required for this book, particularly Rainer Steiman of Zweigart for lovely fabrics, DMC Creative World and Coats Crafts UK for stranded cottons and metallic threads and Ian Lawson Smith for my wonderful cross stitch design programme.

Thanks to Cheryl Brown at David & Charles for continuing to have faith in me, Ame Verso who works on my books and allows me to talk about her remarkable mother, so sadly missed. Linda Clements for her attention to detail and tireless work checking yet another manuscript! A special thank you to Ethan Danielson for his patience, good humour and the excellent stitch diagrams and beautiful charts that make this book so special. Last but not least, my business advisor and guru, Neal Dennis – a special man.

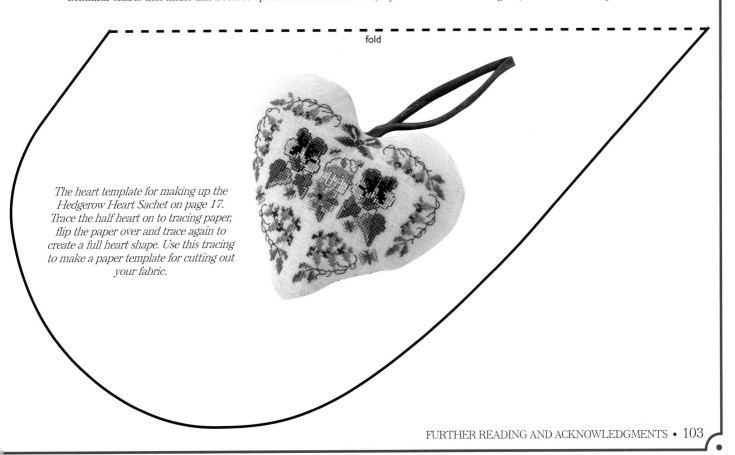

fold

The heart template for making up the Hedgerow Heart Sachet on page 17. Trace the half heart on to tracing paper, flip the paper over and trace again to create a full heart shape. Use this tracing to make a paper template for cutting out your fabric.

Suppliers

UK

If ringing from outside the UK use +44 and no (0)

Artistuff Framing Limited
40–41 Fleet Street, Swindon, Wiltshire SN1 1RE
Tel: +44 (0) 1793 522152
For all the stunning picture frames used in this book

Burford Needlecraft
117 High St, Burford, Oxfordshire OX18 4RG
Tel: +44 (0) 1993 822136
*For general needlework supplies, including Caron threads
(also mail order)*

Coats Crafts UK
PO Box 22, Lingfield Estate, McMullen Road, Darlington,
County Durham, DL1 1YQ
Tel: +44 (0) 1325 365457 (for a list of stockists)
Fax: +44 (0) 1325 338822
*For a wide range of needlework supplies, including
Anchor threads*

The Cross Stitch Guild
Yells Yard, Cirencester Road, Fairford, Gloucestershire
GL7 4BS
Tel: +44 (0) 1285 713799
www.thecrossstitchguild.com
*For a wide range of needlework supplies, including Zweigart
fabrics, threads, handcrafted buttons, cross stitch design
software (Cross Stitch Designer Gold), gold-plated needles
and the USA map sampler chart (see also page 2)*

DMC Creative World Ltd
Pullman Road, Wigston, Leicestershire LE18 2DY
Tel: +44 (0) 116 281 1040
Fax: +44 (0) 116 281 3592
www.dmc.com
*For a wide range of needlework supplies, including
DMC threads*

Lakeland Ltd
Alexandra Buildings, Windermere, Cumbria LA23 1BQ
Tel: +44 (0) 15394 88100
www.lakelandlimited.co.uk
For decorative papers

The Paper Shed
Tollerton, York YO61 1QQ
Tel: +44 (0) 1347 838253
www.papershed.co.uk
For decorative papers

US

Charles Craft Inc
PO Box 1049, Laurenburg, NC 28353
Tel: 910 844 3521
Email: ccraft@carolina.net
www.charlescraft.com
For cross stitch fabrics and many pre-finished items

Kreinik Manufacturing Co Inc
3106 Timanus Lane, Suite 101, Baltimore, Maryland 21244
Tel: 1 800 537 2166 or 1 410 281 0040
Fax: 1 410 281 0987
www.krienik.com
For Kreinik metallic threads and blending filaments

MCG Textiles
13845 Magnolia Avenue, Chino, CA 91710
Tel: 909 591 6351
www.mcgtextiles.com
For cross stitch fabrics and many pre-finished items

M & J Buttons
1000 Sixth Avenue, New York, NY 10018
Tel: 212 391 6200
www.mjtrim.com
For beads, buttons, ribbons and trimmings

Yarn Tree Designs
PO Box 724, Ames, Iowa 500100724
Tel: 1 800 247 3952
www.yarntree.com
For cross stitch supplies and card mounts

Zweigart/Joan Toggit Ltd
262 Old Brunswick Road, Suite E, Piscataway,
NJ 08854-3756
Tel: 732 562 8888
www.zweigart.com
For cross stitch fabrics and linens

Index

Bold indicates technique references

Adam and Eve 13, 38, 46–53
Aida 10, 11, 12, 16, 72, 73, 88
Algerian eye stitch 16, 80, **88**
alphabet samplers 22–9,
    54–61
A Stitch in Time 71, 73, 76–7

backstitch 72, **88**
    outlines 13
    threaded 82, 83, **97**
band samplers 78–87
bars 88, 97
Berlin woolwork 62–9
bias binding 25, **101**
birds, swallows 62–9
blackwork band sampler
    79–80, 84
bookmark, darned 41
border, interlaced 41
Bristol Orphanage sampler
    54–6, 58–9, 61
bullion knots 72, 80, 81
bullion stitch 82, **88–9**
butterflies 17–21, 79, 82, 86,
    99
buttonhole stitch **89**
    detached 81, **89–90**
button loop 25, **89**

cards 33, 40, **101**
caring for samplers 102
carnation and butterfly band
sampler 79, 82, 86
case, stork 73, 99
chain stitch, counted 81, **89**
charts
    Berlin woolwork 65
    personalizing 16, 24
    working from 10, 11, 13,
      88
coasters 41, 72
colour
    shading 64
    single 54–61
cord, twisted 41, **101**
couching 81, 83, **89**
cross stitch **12**, 13
    double 80, **90**

long-legged **94**
    three quarter 12
Cross Stitch Guild 2, 32, 104
cushions 54–5, 57, 60, 101

darning samplers 38–45
design
    personalizing 16, 24, 40,
      48, 73, 76
    size 11
dove's eye stitch 48, 81, **90–1**

edges
    frayed 33, 41, 72, 92
    hemstitched 81, 82, **93**
equipment 10, 104
evenweave 10, 11, 12
eyelets 16, **91**
    half 83, **92**
    quarter 83

fabrics
    choice 10, 83
    preparation 11
finishing work 12, 100–1
flowers
    alphabet sampler 22–9
    band samplers 78–87
    Berlin pictures 64–5
    Berlin swallows sampler
      62–9
    carnation and butterfly
band sampler 79, 82, 86
    floral spray coaster 72
    garden of Eden motif
sampler 46–53
    gardenia darning sampler
      38–45
    heart card 33
    hedgerow heart sachet 17,
      98, 103
    needle fold 24–5, 98
    stitcher's nécessaire 25,
      101
    vase picture 49
    violets and berries band
sampler 79, 83, 87
    wild hedgerow house

sampler 14–21
four-sided stitch 81, 83, **91**
frames, embroidery 10
framing work 100–1, 102
French knot 16, 27, 51, 72,
    80, 81, 82, **91–2**

gardenia darning sampler
    38–45

hearts 17, 33, 81, 98, 103
hemstitch 41, 48, 81, 82, 87,
    92–3
    diamond 81, 83, **90**
    ladder 81, 83, **93**
    zigzag 57, 81, **97**
herringbone stitch 80, 81, **93**
history of samplers 4, 6–9
    links to the past 21, 27,
      35, 49, 61, 80
Holbein stitch 80, **93**
Home Sweet Home 71–2,
    74–5
hoops 10
house samplers 14–21, 99

linen 10

map samplers 8, 30–7, 102
materials 10, 104
measurements 10
miniature samplers 57
Montenegrin stitch 83, **94**
moth damage 102
motif samplers 6–7, 46–53
mounting work 100, 102

needle fold 24–5, 98
needlelace 82, **94–5**
needle roll 49
needles 10
needleweaving 83, 87, 90, **95**

outlines, backstitch 13

paper samplers 6, 8, 70
Pekinese stitch 83, **95**
personalizing designs 16, 24,

40, 48, 73, 76
pictures 49, 57, 61, 64–5
pulled and drawn thread
designs 48, 81, 82, 83, 87, 92,
    95, 97

queen stitch 16, 81, 82, 83,
    96

red samplers 2, 8, 54–61
restoration 7, 102
reweaving threads 92
Rhodes stitch 80, **96**
    half 16, 81, **92**
ribbon garland needle roll 49
rose, bullion **89**

sachet, heart 17, 98, 103
satin stitch 16, 48, 82, **96**
    pulled **95**
scissors 10
shading 64
ships 33–7
spot motif samplers 6–7,
    46–53
starting work 11, 13, 88
stitcher's nécessaire 25, 101
stitch library 88–97
storing samplers 102
stork case 73, 99
strawberries and cream band
sampler 79, 81, 85
stretching work 100
suppliers 104

techniques 11–13
threads 4, 9, 10, 13, 62, 65
tipsy stitch 81, 82, **97**

Vandyke stitch 83, **97**
Victorian sentiments 70–7
violets and berries band
sampler 79, 83, 87

washing 102
wise words samplers 8, 49,
    70–7
working methods 13, 88